by Aimee Cebulski

Kickstarter™ For Dummies®

Published by
John Wiley & Sons, Inc.
111 River Street, Hoboken
NJ 07030-5774

www.wiley.com

About the Author

Aimee Cebulski is a lifelong traveler and recently used Kickstarter to fund her own book, *The Finding 40 Project* (www.finding40.net). She has worked as a freelance travel writer and blogger for the last 15 years. *The Finding 40 Project* combined Cebulski's passion for telling stories through photos and sharing lessons learned from those she has met around the world.

She has had pieces featured in publications such as *Travelhoppers, Scuba Diving Magazine, AdWeek, The Riverside Press-Enterprise, The Arizona Daily Star, Ranch & Coast Magazine, San Diego News Network, The Orange County Register, The Minnesota Star Tribune,* and *Los Angeles Family Magazine,* among others.

Dedication

This book is dedicated to all the Kickstarters out there — pursue your passions, dreams, and ideas, and make them happen!

Author's Acknowledgments

This book would not be possible without the support of my friends and family who helped make my Kickstarter campaign a reality. Thank you to Margot for encouraging me to do this book — and everyone I have worked with to gather this content, especially the *For Dummies* team for their patience and assistance!

Publisher's Acknowledgments

Acquisitions Editor: Amy Fandrei

Senior Project Editor: Rebecca Huehls

Senior Copy Editor: Barry Childs-Helton

Technical Editor: Leah Jones

Editorial Assistant: Annie Sullivan

Senior Editorial Assistant: Cherie Case

Senior Project Coordinator: Kristie Rees

Cover Image: © mbbirdy / iStockphoto

Table of Contents

Introduction.. *1*

About This Book 1
How This Book Is Organized 2
Foolish Assumptions 2
Icons Used in This Book... 3
Where to Go from Here 3

Chapter 1: Introducing Kickstarter................... 5

Looking at the Concept of Crowdfunding............................ 5
Understanding How Funding on Kickstarter Works.............. 7
Recognizing the Advantages of Kickstarter........................ 8
Knowing What Kickstarter Does and Doesn't Fund............. 10
Reading the Fine Print Before You Start 12
Reading through the FAQ 12
Going to Kickstarter's virtual school 14
Following Kickstarter's guidelines.............................. 14
Discovering the Crowdfunding Process............................ 15

Chapter 2: Laying the Foundation for Your Kickstarter Campaign 19

Transforming Your Passion into a Kickstarter Project....... 20
Prepping to Start Your Project................................ 21
What Makes Your Project Unique? Writing a
Short Project Description 24
Creating the Long Project Description................................ 26
Choosing media to support your description........... 27
Risks and Challenges... 28
Making a Compelling Video 29
Outlining the content for your video 29
Choosing tools to make a great video....................... 30
Understanding Kickstarter Categories.................................. 35
Introducing the categories 35
Choosing the right category.. 42
iPhone Elevation Dock: Realizing a Market Niche 43

Chapter 3: Deciding How Much to Ask For 47

Figuring How Much Your Project Will Cost.......................... 47
Outlining broad expense categories 48
Listing individual expenses 49
Trying to estimate those costs 50
Examining other Kickstarter campaigns.................... 54

Estimating Potential Donations.. 57
Who you gonna call? 58
Evaluate your potential reward levels 59
Rewarding your backers... 61
The Order of the Stick: Building on a Fan Base
and Offering Creative Rewards.. 64
Building on a fan base.. 67
Getting creative with rewards.................................... 69
Throwing in the perks.. 71

Chapter 4: Creating a Realistic Timeline 73

Creating a Timeline for Your Campaign............................... 75
Staggering the Reward Dates.. 78
Experiencing Success and Then Delays 79
iPhone Elevation Dock 79
Pebble E-Paper Watch... 80

Chapter 5: Setting Up Your Campaign 83

Kickstarting Your Kickstarter Account................................ 84
Filling Out Your Project Profile 86
Setting Up Backer Rewards... 90
Telling Your Project's Story 91
Uploading your video.. 91
Filling out your project description 92
Adding Details about You 93
Activating Your Payment Account 94
Preparing for Kickstarter Review... 96
Double-checking your campaign uploads 96
Conducting a final review and submitting
your campaign... 96

Chapter 6: Managing an Active Campaign 99

Launching Your Campaign... 99
Creating a Compelling Call to Action................................. 102
Contacting Potential Backers 102
Sending personal e-mails 103
Posting on Facebook 104
Using a Facebook business page 107
Tweeting about your campaign 108
Posting your campaign video on video-sharing
sites... 110
Tracking Your Backers... 111
Contacting Your Backers through Kickstarter................. 113
Sending a message... 113
Posting updates 114
Promoting Your Deadline 117

Paying to Promote Your Campaign 119
    Buying advertising on Facebook............................. 120
    Purchasing other Internet or newspaper ads 121
    Using promotional events and ideas to drive
        backers to your campaign 123
iPhone Elevation Dock: Getting the Word Out 125
Finding 40: Learning from My Own Kickstarter
    Campaign(s)... 127
    Looking at my project 127
    Filling the content... 128
    Failing to use my own networks 129
    Not strategizing properly.. 130
    Second campaign: Success!....................................... 130

Chapter 7: Kickstarter for iPhone 133

Downloading the App 134
Logging In and Out.. 136
Touring the Kickstarter App Interface 137
    Discovering projects 137
    Checking other projects' activities............................ 138
    Peeking into your profile 139
Managing Your Campaign from the Kickstarter App 140
    Viewing and replying to messages 140
    Seeing your account activity..................................... 141
    Posting project updates for your backers................ 142

Chapter 8: Seeing the Light at the End
of Your Campaign 145

Handling a Struggling or Unsuccessful Campaign 145
Thanking Your Backers 147
Building a Community around Your Project 148
    Sustaining the community after your project ends..... 148
    Fostering your community offline 149
Delivering Rewards to Your Backers................................. 151
    Downloading your Backer Report 151
    Surveying your backers 154
Keeping Up with Kickstarter... 157

Chapter 9: Ten Unique Reward Ideas 159

"Cover Me!": Featuring Backers on Your Cover 159
"The Shirt Off Your Back": Offering T-Shirts 161
"Naming Rights": Including a Backer as a Character......... 162
"Autograph, Please": Signing Your Work 163
"Casting Call": Rewarding Backers with Bit Parts.............. 164
"Curtain Call": Sharing Tickets to Your Show 165

"Hero Worship": Making a Backer the Hero of Your
Project 166
"Dinner Guest": Meeting Your Backers in Person............. 167
"Sign Me Up": Offering Subscriptions................................. 169
"Fly Me to the Moon": Bringing an Out-of-Town
Backer to an Event 170

**Chapter 10: Ten Resources to Help
with Your Campaign.........................173**

Finding Kickstarter-Specific Resources............................. 173
Learning from Other Kickstarter Stories 175
Budgeting for Your Project.. 176
Making a Business Plan.. 177
Writing Well 179
Copywriting Well... 180
Writing Press Releases 182
Building a Basic Website.. 185
WordPress.com... 187
Blogger 190
Tumblr.. 191
Taking Great Photos 191
Promoting Your Project or Event 192

Index... *194*

Introduction

● ●

Kickstarter has gone from a small startup Internet company in 2009 to one of the leading tools used to fund tens of thousands of creative projects. The company uses a concept called *crowdfunding*, or bringing together many people to support a concept, product, or idea. Crowdfunding works by allowing individuals to provide financial backing to a project they want to see come to fruition.

However, Kickstarter is different from other types of fundraising-oriented platforms. The people posting campaigns are not asking for donations for a favorite charity or cause; they are asking backers to believe in their *idea*. Kickstarter has quickly become a mainstream way to get a creative project made, whether it's backing for a feature or documentary film or preselling copies of a book. According to a July 2012 report in *Publishers Weekly,* Kickstarter has already revolutionized the graphic novel industry, quickly becoming the second-largest publisher for this type of work.

Everyone from Academy Award–winning writers to long-established musical acts are using Kickstarter to get their latest projects off the ground without waiting for a studio or publisher to come along. Thanks to the nature of digital giving (using a credit card over the Internet), backers can come from anywhere and support projects at any level, from $1 to $10,000 and beyond.

About This Book

This book is mostly for anyone considering — or in the process of — raising money for a project via a Kickstarter campaign. You find a little bit of information about backing projects and an introduction to what Kickstarter is all about, too, but the book's focus is squarely on raising funds through Kickstarter.

Whether your project is just a spark of an idea or a fully conceived one for which you simply need the funds, this book can help you with your Kickstarter campaign. This book will give you a step-by-step guide to conceptualizing your Kickstarter campaign, gathering the pieces needed and tools available to maximize your push, as well as deciding what to do after your project is funded.

I offer tips to help you accomplish your goals at every stage in the process: determining how much to ask for, managing your campaign throughout the fundraising timeframe, and more. Throughout the book, you also find case studies about successful campaigns and how they applied concepts I explain in a chapter.

Kickstarter is a powerful tool — not only to raise funds for your idea or project, but also to create a community. The Kickstarter website has tools for backer updates, links to Facebook, and opportunities to be seen by other enthusiasts in your neighborhood or category. I help you identify ways to use these tools for sharing your idea with a large, previously untapped audience.

How This Book Is Organized

This book begins with chapters that cover the basics of Kickstarter, including how the site's all-or-nothing approach works and a history of some of the most successful campaigns.

The middle chapters address the process for creating your campaign, uploading content, and getting approved.

The last chapters look at what to do after your project is funded and offer a list of ideas for unique backer rewards.

Foolish Assumptions

I assume in writing this book that you know the basics of how to use a computer and the Internet, as well as basic communication tools like e-mail and Facebook. I also assume you understand the basics of loading photos and videos up to the Internet and the idea of dragging-and-dropping elements in a program.

However, I do not assume to know why you are using Kickstarter. I don't know about your project, your hopes, and goals. My goal is to give you the tools needed to create a successful Kickstarter campaign and transform your idea into reality.

Icons Used in This Book

I use some basic icons throughout this book to help you quickly scan and find useful information and tips.

When you see the Tip icon, you're getting a quick tidbit of handy information on using Kickstarter.

Some information is important to remember as you use Kickstarter, so when you see this Remember icon, be sure to tuck the information away for future reference.

Watch out! As with any online tool, you might need to avoid some pitfalls or do a vital task as you participate. Also, because Kickstarter is always changing, I alert you to some potential issues in advance.

Where to Go from Here

The simplest route is to read this book in order, from beginning to end, but that certainly isn't mandatory. If you're brand new to Kickstarter or will be setting up your account as you read this book, I recommend reading the chapters in order. After you read this book, keep it handy and use it as a reference as you navigate Kickstarter.

Please keep in mind that web interfaces can change at any moment and without notice. The overall concepts in this book apply no matter how Kickstarter or the other tools mentioned throughout this book change their interfaces. So please know that we checked that all the information in this book was accurate as the book went to press, but some minor details in the steps and the way the websites look are likely to change. For major updates related to the book, you can also check out this book's web page at www.dummies.com/go/kickstarterfdupdates.

Chapter 1

Introducing Kickstarter

"*I* get by with a little help from my friends. . . ." It's a line from one of the Beatles' most popular songs but also a mantra for millions. People seek help for everything — and many great communities and companies are built thanks to the generosity of a group of people, all working toward a common goal.

That concept has been frequently translated to charitable endeavors. How often have you been asked to donate $5 for a bake sale or $25 for a fundraising walk? When you hear statistics about millions being raised for a charity through a race or telethon, it's because a large group of people backed the charity — some on a large scale at a high level, some on a smaller scale at a more modest level. The essential idea, though, is that a large group of people backed a cause. Whatever was done was done by a crowd.

This phenomenon has a name — *crowdfunding* — and it's one of the essential concepts behind Kickstarter. In the sections that follow, you learn what crowdfunding and Kickstarter are all about, discover their advantages, and how Kickstarter specifically uses the crowdfunding concept to help people with funding their creative projects.

Looking at the Concept of Crowdfunding

Crowdfunding is not a new idea. As I mention earlier, countless charity organizations have used crowds to meet their fundraising goals.

You even see crowdfunding on a very basic level in most households. Each member contributes something to the overall success of the house. Dad contributes X, Mom contributes Y, kids contribute Z. Together, the crowd makes the house work, and unlike donating to a charity out of the goodness of your heart, people involved in this scenario want something out of their backing. In this case, all the members of the household work together to benefit from a stable residence, protection from the elements, and a sense of community.

Kickstarter was born in 2009 to help creative people get their projects made with the support of many ("a crowd") while promising these backers something in return. It's not an altruistic model. People back the projects with the expectation that they will get something for their money.

Unlike a traditional process of trying to prove your concept to a movie studio, publisher, or agent, people are using Kickstarter to have their own network of friends, business and professional associates, industry peers, and family validate their concept by backing the project — in a way, judging whether it will be successful before it is even distributed.

This model is revolutionizing many aspects of business, with creative people from all walks of life turning to Kickstarter to make their projects into realities without waiting for an industry insider to give it the green light.

A brief history of Kickstarter

In 2001, Perry Chen was a musician living in New Orleans. He wanted to create an event that would dovetail into the city's famous Jazz Festival — but he didn't have the funds to put on something of this scale by himself. He ended up not trying to fund the event himself, but it got him thinking about the idea of asking a group to back an event or program, trying to make something happen.

It wasn't until 2009, after he met up with co-founders Yancey Strickler and Charles Adler in New York, that Kickstarter was born.

In the last three years, the company has grown exponentially, creating a viable tool for creative types to make their dreams into realities.

The model seems to be working. As of March 2013, individuals using Kickstarter have

- ✔ Launched 89,400 projects
- ✔ Funded 37,300 projects — a success rate of 43%
- ✔ Raised $434 million

Understanding How Funding on Kickstarter Works

The number of launched projects on Kickstarter (89,400 and count-ing, as I write this chapter) is much larger than the number of suc-cessfully funded projects (37,300). What does that mean?

Kickstarter uses an all-or-nothing approach to fundraising. This means, if you don't hit your fundraising goal within a certain time-frame (about 30 to 60 days), you get *nothing*. As a result, you need to be very strategic in your planning, goal-setting, and backer solicitation, all of which I cover in depth in this book.

When you launch a Kickstarter project, your fundraising hap-pens via your Kickstarter campaign page. Potential backers see a description of your concept, your fundraising goal, and an assortment of backer rewards which you determine. A potential backer chooses his or level of support for your project; that per-son's pledge goes toward your goal. Figure 1-1 shows an active Kickstarter campaign page, where you can see such details as the project's video, funding goal, and days remaining.

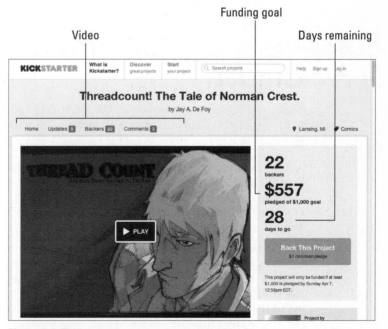

Figure 1-1: This campaign page shows the video, funding goal, and days remaining.

Over the weeks, your dollars raised will increase and your amount to reach your goal will decrease (ideally) each day until your campaign is over.

Kickstarter makes its money by taking a percentage (or fee) from your funds raised. Similar to a marketing fee, you are basically paying a commission to Kickstarter to use its website to promote your campaign. If your Kickstarter campaign is successfully funded, Kickstarter will take 5 percent of your final total for its fee.

However, if you come to the end of your Kickstarter campaign and have not reached your project goal, you *do not receive any of the pledges listed to date.* You have to raise your minimum goal amount to receive any of your backer pledges. You also do not pay anything to Kickstarter, since your campaign was not successful.

In this book, I explain how to prepare for your Kickstarter campaign so that you're well-positioned for funding success. It's also important to remember that Kickstarter is designed to get your project up and running, and you need to have a plan after your Kickstarter campaign is over. Chapter 10 looks at some of the tools available for creating a business plan for your project, setting yourself up for the opportunity to sustain your project after the campaign is over, and for making money in the future.

Recognizing the Advantages of Kickstarter

You might be a little intimidated by an all-or-nothing approach, and by the prospect of asking backers to help you reach your goal. However, this model has advantages for both you and your backers:

- ✓ **A firm deadline forces you to focus on your campaign and on soliciting backers:** If you weren't working against the clock, you might be tempted to wait around to see what backers come in, instead of actively soliciting support. This format encourages you to move your project along quickly.

- ✓ **The all-or-nothing approach is less of a risk to your backers:** Since nothing gets funded if the project does not reach its goal (that is, prove its value), backers don't have to worry about supporting a potentially losing project. They know their accounts will not be charged unless a lot of other people also believe in the idea.

Kickstarter also makes it easy to spread the word about your project and build community:

- ✔ **Backers can share their passion for a project with a click of the mouse:** Because your fundraising happens online, backers can encourage others to get behind an idea through a Facebook or Twitter post that includes a link to your campaign page. Likewise, bloggers and journalists can boost awareness of your campaign and send potential backers your way with a link on their own blogs or websites. For example, Figure 1-2 shows a post about the Caravan Pacific Kickstarter campaign; the post appeared on the popular blog, Design Sponge.

- ✔ **Using Kickstarter to get your project off the ground truly creates a sense of community:** Your backers feel like they are really making it happen and are often thrilled to get in on the ground floor of something.

Figure 1-2: Example of how word can spread with just a click of the mouse.

- ✔ **You retain creative control over your project:** In the past, if you wanted to create a film, art show, project, or play, you needed financial backers. That might mean investors or a publisher or a studio behind you. The advantage was that potentially one major investor might give you the funds needed to make your concept come to life — but also exert influence and pressure to change your project to meet his or her specifications. You would gain a backer, but you might end up losing creative control.

One of Kickstarter's greatest advantages is that you can still solicit the backing needed to get your project off the ground, but you maintain complete creative control, delivering a product that matches your vision.

Kim Krizan, writer of hit movies, *Before Sunrise* and *Before Sunset,* knew Kickstarter was the right vehicle for her when she wrote a tongue-in-cheek book about a femme fatale and wanted to produce it on her own terms.

Being a successful, established writer, she said on her Kickstarter page that she could "just get it into the hands of a publisher . . . I could also put it online and be done with it. But I thought it would be so much cooler to take it directly to you." She decided to use her audience to make the project happen without the pressure of a publisher.

As shown in Figure 1-3, Krizan secured 183 backers and beat her $10,000 goal by almost $1,000, so she's on her way!

Figure 1-3: Successful Kickstarter campaign page for *Original Sins: Trade Secrets of a Femme Fatale.*

Knowing What Kickstarter Does and Doesn't Fund

Unlike other web-based tools soliciting funds, Kickstarter is not a fundraising tool for charity.

Kickstarter is for projects *only,* not causes or fundraising drives. Your campaign must be for a specific creative project or concept. If your campaign is determined to be a charity fundraiser, the Kickstarter team will deny your application.

Along those same lines, Kickstarter does not allow "Fund My Life" projects. You cannot have an open-ended campaign to raise money for a trip to Bora Bora or help you fund a sabbatical. Kickstarter campaigns are for specific projects and costs.

If it appears your Kickstarter campaign is to fund a vacation or allow you to quit your job, it will be denied.

Kickstarter also doesn't allow certain types of content, such as knives, real estate, bath and beauty products, and nutritional supplements. This means projects such as ReadyCase, an iPhone case that includes a multitool with regular and serrated blades, as shown in Figure 1-4, wouldn't have been a good fit for Kickstarter, even though it's a legitimate project. The creators of this case chose a different crowdfunding site called Indiegogo.

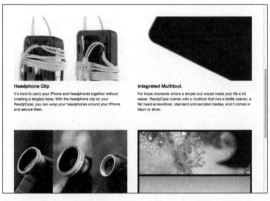

Figure 1-4: Example of a project that would not meet Kickstarter guidelines.

Indiegogo differs most clearly from Kickstarter on one key issue: It's not an all-or-nothing approach. Indiegogo has several models that allow you to keep your backer pledges even if you don't reach your goal, for a higher fee.

For the full list of content Kickstarter does and doesn't allow, check out the Prohibited Uses section of the Kickstarter guidelines at www.kickstarter.com/help/guidelines. The next section goes into more detail about how you can familiarize yourself with Kickstarter's terms and conditions.

Reading the Fine Print Before You Start

Before you launch or back a campaign on Kickstarter, you need to make sure it's a good fit for the site and understand *all* the terms and conditions. As I mention in the preceding section, you won't get far on Kickstarter if your project doesn't meet Kickstarter's guidelines. You must also meet Kickstarter's residency requirements. (You must live in the U.S. or the U.K. and meet certain requirements in each country.) And don't forget, if your campaign is successful, Kickstarter takes a 5 percent cut of your funds, which is how the website stays in business.

Of course, you probably bought this book because you're eager to get started on raising the funds for your project. But you'll do yourself a huge favor if you read all the details and requirements first. If your campaign is successful, you've most likely started a small business for yourself, even if you don't plan to run it forever. That comes with certain commitments to Kickstarter, your backers, and your tax bill.

In the following sections, I point you to the key areas of the Kickstarter site that help you become familiar with Kickstarter's terms and the responsibilities you take on if your campaign is successful. I also point you to features on the Kickstarter site that help you run a successful campaign.

To find these tools, click the What Is Kickstarter? link at the top of the Kickstarter home page, as shown in Figure 1-5.

Reading through the FAQ

For a quick snapshot of all the parts of Kickstarter, click the FAQ (Frequently Asked Questions) link, and you see the page shown in Figure 1-6. Here you see three main sections:

- **Kickstarter Basics:** Discusses the concept behind the website, how you might use it, your responsibilities as a Kickstarter user, and getting involved with other Kickstarter projects.

- **Creator Questions:** An overview of the main things you have to keep in mind and remember as you plan, upload, and launch a Kickstarter campaign.

✔ **Backer Questions:** Are you considering backing another Kickstarter project? This section shows the top questions and issues when it comes to pledging money to support another Kickstarter project.

Click to see FAQ, guidelines, and more

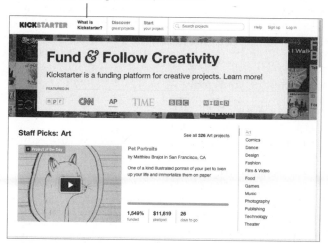

Figure 1-5: Click the What Is Kickstarter? link to find help and guidelines.

Main FAQ categories

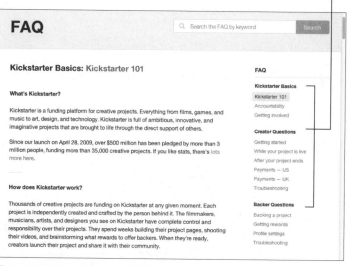

Figure 1-6: A list of the main FAQ categories.

Going to Kickstarter's virtual school

Attending Kickstarter's virtual school, shown in Figure 1-7, can help get you oriented right away. Kickstarter School is just what it sounds like — sections of the site presented in a classroom or textbook style, showing the main steps of launching a Kickstarter campaign:

1. Defining your project

2. Creating rewards

3. Setting your goal

4. Making your video

5. Building your project

6. Promoting your project

7. Project updates

8. Reward fulfillment

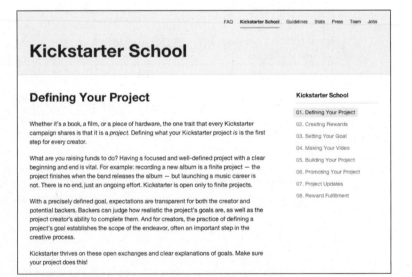

Figure 1-7: A look at the topics in the Kickstarter School.

Following Kickstarter's guidelines

Earlier in this chapter, I discuss how Kickstarter — works and offer an overview of its guidelines. When you click the Guidelines link, you see a comprehensive list of all things to take into consideration when planning a potential Kickstarter campaign (as shown in Figure 1-8), including community guidelines.

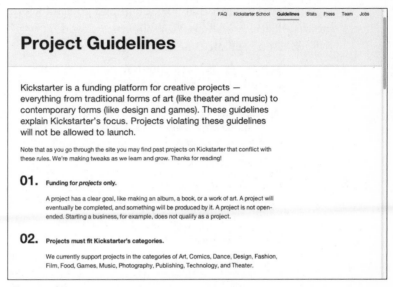

FAQ   Kickstarter School   **Guidelines**   Stats   Press   Team   Jobs

Project Guidelines

Kickstarter is a funding platform for creative projects — everything from traditional forms of art (like theater and music) to contemporary forms (like design and games). These guidelines explain Kickstarter's focus. Projects violating these guidelines will not be allowed to launch.

Note that as you go through the site you may find past projects on Kickstarter that conflict with these rules. We're making tweaks as we learn and grow. Thanks for reading!

01. Funding for *projects* only.

A project has a clear goal, like making an album, a book, or a work of art. A project will eventually be completed, and something will be produced by it. A project is not open-ended. Starting a business, for example, does not qualify as a project.

02. Projects must fit Kickstarter's categories.

We currently support projects in the categories of Art, Comics, Dance, Design, Fashion, Film, Food, Games, Music, Photography, Publishing, Technology, and Theater.

Figure 1-8: A look at the comprehensive guidelines.

Discovering the Crowdfunding Process

Running a successful Kickstarter campaign is a lot of work, but most of it is the fun kind of work because you're doing it to support your passion and creative idea. The following steps walk you through the overall process of a Kickstarter campaign and point you to the chapters where you find out more about each phase of the process:

1. **Make sure you have a clearly defined project.**

   To start, you need to make sure your idea is clear and unique. Then you need to figure out how to communicate why your project needs to be made in a straightforward and succinct way to your backers. You find help doing just that in Chapter 2.

2. **Figure out what your fundraising goal should be and how much your rewards need to cost in order to meet that goal.**

Because Kickstarter requires you to ask for a certain amount of money, you have to figure out the minimum amount of money you need to cover the costs of creating your project — and the different levels of donations you need to meet that goal. Chapter 3 goes into detail about building an accurate budget.

3. **Set a realistic timeline.**

Kickstarter requires you to raise your funds in a certain amount of time, and your backers will also want to know when they'll receive the rewards you're offering. Your campaign and your relationship with your backers will go much more smoothly if you think through your timeline in advance. In Chapter 4, I lay out some suggestions on how to build a timeline that works for both you and your backers, taking into account such factors as troubleshooting possible delays, handling holidays, and watching out for industry factors that might influence your planning process.

4. **Prepare your campaign and submit it for Kickstarter review and approval.**

Steps 1–3 are all up-front work. You want to make sure you've thought through the important details before you start developing your campaign page through Kickstarter's dashboard for project creators. This step is where you take all the content and data you've been developing and enter it into what amounts to a proposal that Kickstarter will review. If your project meets all of Kickstarter's requirements, you receive an e-mail that Kickstarter has approved your project. Chapter 5 walks you through each part of the Kickstarter project setup process and gives you helpful tips to ensure that your project makes it through the review process smoothly.

5. **Launch your campaign and promote your project on a day-to-day basis.**

You can't just launch your campaign and hope for the best. To reach your funding goal, you need to reach out to friends, family, and your personal and professional communities. You also need to promote your deadline. Chapter 6 helps you stay on top of all the key tools, both online and elsewhere, that help you reach out to potential backers and the backers you gain throughout your campaign. Chapter 7 orients you to the tools in the Kickstarter-sponsored iPhone app that help you manage an active campaign while you're on the go.

6. Stay in touch with backers as you create your project and deliver backer rewards.

Remember, when you get to the end of your Kickstarter campaign, that doesn't mean your project is over — far from it! Your backers have invested their own money in your project and are likely interested to hear how it's going. You have a unique opportunity to continue building community among your backers as you create your project. You also have to manage the nuts and bolts of delivering the rewards you promised your backers in a timely manner. Kickstarter has tools to help you with all these, and in Chapter 8, I walk you through the steps of using each one. You also find my tips for finishing your campaign and building upon it to ensure long-term success.

In Chapter 9, you find ten unique reward ideas, and in Chapter 10, ten resources beyond Kickstarter that can help you throughout the stages of your Kickstarter campaign. Each of these chapters gives you even more ammunition for Kickstarter success!

Chapter 2

Laying the Foundation for Your Kickstarter Campaign

In This Chapter

▶ Getting your project ready for crowdfunding

▶ Highlighting what makes your project unique

▶ Writing your project description to appeal to supporters

▶ Making the best use of Kickstarter categories

*O*ne of the biggest challenges (and also opportunities) with Kickstarter is deciding what your unique project will be, determining what makes it special, and then labeling it in the appropriate category.

In this chapter, I examine ways to think about framing your project and communicating what makes it unique, and also determining its appropriate Kickstarter category.

In order to create a winning and engaging campaign, you need to have a dynamic and interesting presence on Kickstarter. Hundreds of projects are added every week, so yours needs to stand out and catch everyone's eye, not just your friends.

In this chapter, I show you how to make a strong impression by carefully choosing your category, writing interesting copy, and creating a compelling video to explain your Kickstarter project. I'll also delve into some of the resources available around the web to make your content as interesting as possible.

Transforming Your Passion into a Kickstarter Project

Your best bet is to have a specific project already in mind. If you just want to use Kickstarter to stimulate your creative juices, that's putting the cart before the horse. Your campaign needs to be concrete and well-rounded, focused on putting a real product out. If you're having trouble figuring out what project is the best fit for your passion, this section can help.

To start, consider the following example: Say you're interested in sharing the story of an amazing disabled athlete who has overcome horrendous injuries and is now competing at the World Triathlete Championships. You know this athlete personally and feel his story of triumph over tragedy could inspire others — but you're unsure about how to proceed.

A first step would be to think about this passion and the best possible way to tell the story. Make a list that examines the following questions:

- ✔ **Is this a story you can tell in real time?** Continuing the earlier example, telling the story in real time means you'll follow the athlete's upcoming competition. A story that's not in real time would have a different focus (say, retelling an amazing past accomplishment).

- ✔ **What kind of material will you have access to and use to tell this story?** For example, will you have video and photos, or just photos? This consideration might help you determine whether your project should be a short film or a photo-gallery showing.

- ✔ **Are you familiar with the project's topic personally, or is it something you'll need to research?** How close are you to a subject? If you don't have a personal relationship with the potential person(s) involved, perhaps seek out opportunities to get to know him or her before beginning the Kickstarter project.

- ✔ **Do you have more experience in one type of project than another?** If you have written many magazine articles and short stories in the past, but have never attempted a short film or documentary, consider researching articles and seminars relating to topics such as "translating a story to film" before you embark on the project.

> ✔ **How many resources would you have at your disposal for each type of project you're considering?** Make a list of every piece of equipment, software program, or other tool you have for each type of project (film, book, showing, whatever); see where the biggest gaps in your list are. Also, think about whether you will need to hire people to help make your project a reality. In Chapter 3, you consider the need to pay for or barter with this outside help.

By examining your responses to all these questions, you can get a clear idea of what it takes to turn your passion into a project. When you know what type of project you want to create, you're ready to start preparing the material for your Kickstarter campaign, as I explain in the next section.

Prepping to Start Your Project

You can save time down the road by preparing key elements of your project information before you begin to set it up on Kickstarter. Figure 2-1 gives you an overview of the elements you need to prepare for your campaign page, which explains your overall vision for your Kickstarter project. The following list introduces each item:

Figure 2-1: An overview of a Kickstarter campaign page.

✔ **A fabulous project name**: The name for your project is critical because it needs to explain what the project is all about. Chose a title that is simple, specific, and memorable. Avoid using words like *help*; such words are too generic. Choose words that exemplify what you're doing *through active terms*. Here are some examples of good project names that are compelling and specific:

- Nomiku: Bring *sous vide* into your kitchen

- Fund the 2013 Union Square Fire Dancing Expo

- *The Goon Movie* — Let's Kickstart this Sucker!

✔ **An image that represents your project:** Kickstarter requires an image in a *4:3 aspect ratio*, meaning that the image is slightly more horizontal than vertical. Also, be sure that the image has a high enough resolution to look good on the World Wide Web — ideally 200 dpi or higher to avoid pixilation.

Choose an image that summarizes your project in a nutshell, like a logo, a photo of your design prototype or book cover, a screen shot from a video (if you're already underway on production), still photos from a studio shoot, and so on. Ideally you won't use just a photo of yourself, but instead something that shows what the project is about.

Your project image needs to grab a viewer's attention and visually illustrate the nature of your project quickly. The image is featured on the Kickstarter main page if someone is searching in your category or geographic region. Figure 2-2 showcases a great project image for the Pebble E-Paper Watch, discussed in this book as the all-time most successful Kickstarter campaign. The image is simple, clean, compelling, and clearly shows the project.

✔ **A short blurb that describes your project:** Think Twitter; think elevator pitch. The limit for your short description is 135 *characters* (not 135 *words*). For pointers on creating an effective description, flip to "What Makes Your Project Unique? Writing a Short Project Description" later in this chapter. The short description will appear just below your photo on your main project page; it should be almost as short as a photo caption. It will also appear with your project image on any category or search pages, as mentioned earlier.

✔ **A short video that grabs attention:** A key element of every Kickstarter project is a short video, ideally two minutes or less. See the section "Making a Compelling Video" later in this chapter for more details.

Pebble E-Paper Watch project image

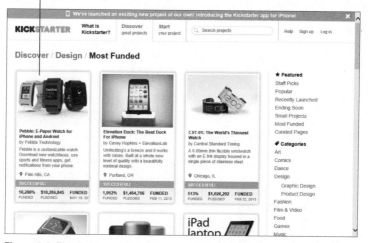

Figure 2-2: The Pebble E-Paper Watch had a great project image for its Kickstarter campaign.

✔ **Duration for your project campaign:** Kickstarter recommends a campaign timeframe of 30 days or less, but doesn't insist upon it. The campaign duration is your call. In fact, several campaigns run up to 60 days. The advantage of a shorter window is a sense of urgency to encourage backers to donate; however, it gives you less time to promote your project. I suggest you check out the details about managing and spreading the word about your campaign (they're in Chapter 6) before you determine your campaign duration.

✔ **A project funding goal:** Before you go online to set up a project, think through your funding needs and have an amount in mind. Setting the funding goal is a big part of any program's success. Chapter 3 goes into detail about how much to ask for, depending on what your project needs.

✔ **A category:** Every Kickstarter project needs to fit into one of the site's defined categories. The section "Understanding Kickstarter Categories" later in this chapter details the available categories and how to classify your project, but think early on about what category your work might fall into.

✔ **Your bio:** You will be asked to write a short description about yourself for your project. If you have an existing bio/CV/résumé completed, locate it and review it before you go any further; think about what elements you want to highlight in your personal Kickstarter bio. Be sure to include any experience or accomplishments you have that demonstrate your ability to meet the goals you've outlined in your campaign.

✔ **A full description of your project:** Beyond the short blurb, you will be writing a detailed description of your campaign, goals, risks, and challenges. The section "Creating the Long Project Description" later in this chapter details the steps needed to fill this out, and it is a good idea to begin outlining the details of your campaign before you go much further.

✔ **Rewards:** Every Kickstarter campaign has backer rewards at several funding levels. Even if you're unsure about your own potential rewards at this point, take a quick browse through other campaigns on the site to get an idea of the types of reward levels out there. You find out more about rewards in Chapters 3 and 9.

What Makes Your Project Unique? Writing a Short Project Description

Your short project description needs to convey your project's *unique selling point.* This may sound a bit like a marketing term, and in a way, it is. This description appears just below your main project image on your campaign home page and on any search pages. You only get 135 characters (this includes spaces) in these areas of the Kickstarter site to make your project stand out.

Tens of thousands of books, movies, comic books, games, and products are marketed every year. Your Kickstarter project is no different. A strong unique selling point helps you

✔ Create a concise project description.

✔ Describe your project quickly to potential backers.

✔ Differentiate your project from the thousands of others on the market.

The following steps can help you pinpoint what makes your project unique in your short product description:

1. **Describe your project in one word: film, book, show, design, product, painting, and so on.**

   This single-word description helps you get at the very core of the project and gets you thinking about how to differentiate from other ideas.

2. **Build a powerful phrase or sentence around your one word.**

   For example: *A film about families struggling to overcome poverty in rural America.*

   This expanded phrase explains the core of the project.

3. **Expand your sentence so that it explains why your project is different or better than others on the market:**

   Unlike previous documentaries that only show the nuts-and-bolts basics of the fiscal impact of poverty in rural America, this film will go deeper, examining the specific psychological effects long-term poverty has on rural families.

4. **Check the character count of your sentence. In Microsoft Word, you can do this by selecting the text and clicking the word count in the lower-left corner of the screen.**

   When you click the word count, a Word Count dialog box appears with additional details including the character count without spaces and the character count with spaces. Most other word processing programs offer a similar tool.

5. **If you're not within the 135-character limit, start by deleting any unnecessary words and looking for phrases that you can make more concise by replacing them with single words.**

   In the example just given, the description is beyond 135 characters (spaces count for characters). If the differentiating quality of the film is psychological effects versus fiscal impact, you might narrow down the description as follows:

   Documentaries about poor rural American families usually focus on money. This film examines poverty's deep psychological effects.

   This new description is only 130 characters, including spaces.

You may find yourself struggling a bit here, determining how to phrase your expanded sentence and short unique selling proposition. Practice describing your project in a succinct way a few different times. After you edit down the description as needed, read and re-read the description. Create multiple versions with different lead-ins until you find the right mix.

If you find you cannot describe your project quickly and accurately, perhaps you have too vague of a concept. Think about what you want to focus on, and then ask the following questions (each sample question is followed by a real-world example):

✔ **Is there a way I can limit the time duration of my project?** Instead of following an athlete for an entire year on his or her journey, should I only focus on a three-month window?

✔ **Should I focus on a specific geographic area?** Is it too ambitious to document all the taco shops in California? Should I only focus on one region, such as Southern California?

✔ **Is my finished product too long?** Would this film about a symphony be better as a short documentary instead of a full-length one?

✔ **Would this concept be building on (or redoing) something already in the market? If so, how? Where will my project take the concept?** How is this iPhone accessory different from the hundreds of others already on Kickstarter?

✔ **Can I eliminate an element of my project?** Do I need to make three versions of my comic book? Should I only produce one?

✔ **Should I collaborate with someone else to make the project more complete or understandable?** If I partner with a videographer, can we make a combination web series and documentary at the same time to make a more compelling finished product?

Start with whatever notes you have for your unique selling proposition. Then go through and answer each of these questions individually. Expand or contract your unique selling proposition based on your responses. Then try rewording it.

Creating the Long Project Description

On your campaign page, your *long project description* appears below the short blurb. This long project description is your opportunity to tell the full story of your passion and reasoning behind your Kickstarter campaign. Although you aren't limited by a certain number of characters, it's best to first revisit the initial description that you started when you were writing your short blurb. Go back to that first sentence you were writing, and instead of trying to cut it down to 135 characters, look at how you can expand on it:

✔ Write as if you were talking to a friend about how your passion got started.

✔ Use a conversational tone, so potential backers get a sense of what you're like.

✔ Use at least 3–4 sentences to describe *why* you want to make your project.

✔ In as much detail as possible, describe the steps of your project and various milestones you hope to accomplish.

✔ Similar to when you wrote your short blurb, clearly define how your project is different from others and why a backer should pledge. In addition to text, you have many opportunities to apply formatting and add additional media. Use the Bold, Underline, and Italic formatting buttons to draw attention to specific elements of your campaign or key milestones.

You can also link to other web pages or content here as well. If you want potential backers to learn more about the issue or topic associated with your project, insert the appropriate web links.

Choosing media to support your description

Media is the key to keeping attention here! In the Project Description box, you can add pictures, audio, and more video to support your idea.

I would recommend adding specific media here to help tell your story. You might have used these already in your Project Video, but it doesn't hurt to reinforce your story and also give potential backers quick information that they can browse without watching the entire video:

✔ Photos of your project in action (if available)

✔ Photos related to your topic and supporting visuals

✔ Short audio clips — especially helpful if you're a musician and have a demo track or sample of how your project sounds

✔ Video clips from your project (if available)

✔ Photos or video clips from any press interviews you may have done

Keep all your clips in this section short, ideally 20 to 30 seconds or fewer. You want potential backers to get a sense of the campaign and your specific points, but keep in mind that they have a lot of content to go through!

Risks and Challenges

The project description also includes a section called Risks and Challenges. This special section lets you address what issues you think might come up during your project and how you plan to address them. In short, this gives your backers some peace of mind when they ask, "Does this person have the ability to pull this project off?" or even more importantly, "Do I feel confident giving this person my money, sure that he or she will deliver the item in the campaign as promised?"

Unhappy Kickstarter backers tend to be very vocal about over-due rewards, production delays, and changes. Especially if your campaign includes a lot of variables that might be out of your control, be sure to use this section to highlight the potential pit-falls clearly and how you are anticipating overcoming them. The last thing you want is a bunch of unhappy backers posting about delays on social media!

In order to best fill out this box, go back to your project budget and review all the parts required to make your campaign a suc-cess. Which elements do you think might present the biggest obstacles?

Here are a few examples of such challenges:

- ✔ Unable to get required raw material (such as video footage, usable images, interview audio) to complete the project
- ✔ Running out of time or missing deadlines
- ✔ Conflicts with weather/seasons/special events
- ✔ Personal time constraints
- ✔ Production delays
- ✔ Lack of knowledge or technical skill
- ✔ Budget overages

For each bullet item you think of for your individual campaign, come up with at least one (ideally two) responses that show how you will handle each problem.

Combine the potential challenges and solutions list into a para-graph or two and paste it here. By addressing these issues early, you get used to thinking about what you might need to have in place before even launching your campaign — and about how to assure your backers that you have the skills needed to handle the challenges. This early, proactive thinking builds community with your backers for the long haul.

Making a Compelling Video

Your video is featured at the very top of your Kickstarter campaign page — and needs to draw in potential backers quickly.

Before even starting your project, it's best to spend time creating the video and getting it ready for upload.

 A polished video eases the approval process (in which Kickstarter reviews your overall project application). If your video flows smoothly, has a good look and feel, and accurately explains your project, the Kickstarter review team can see that you understand the guidelines and requirements for a campaign. If your video is unfinished or hard to follow, it may be harder for Kickstarter to see that your campaign fits its requirements.

In the following sections, you explore what content to include in your video and basic tools for creating a video.

Outlining the content for your video

The video is one of the most important tools you have to get backers excited about your Kickstarter campaign. Why? The video tells a story in an easy-to-follow way and doesn't require backers to go through lines of text.

Your video needs to specifically address your Kickstarter campaign. Be sure you clearly convey the primary goal of your campaign. For example, is the campaign hoping to completely fund a new fashion item and get it in stores, or provide resources to make samples for a trunk show? As you gather your raw materials outlined later in this section, constantly think about how each element will illustrate the goal of your campaign. If it doesn't fit, don't use it. A hilarious photo of your product idea in some fantastical scene doesn't necessarily belong in your Kickstarter video. Even if humorous, your video needs to be professional and convey a clear message to instill confidence in your backers.

An important element to consider when beginning your Project Video: Two minutes or less! Why two minutes or less? Internet users, even those seeking creative projects and content, have an extremely short attention span. An average commercial is 30 seconds; an average television news segment is two and a half minutes. If you can't tell the story of your project in under two minutes, it's unlikely you will be able to draw backers in.

Before beginning production of your video, gather up and identify the raw materials you might want to include, such as

- ✔ Existing video clips of your project underway, if available

- ✔ Still photos from your project underway, if available

- ✔ Still photos of prototypes, samples, or examples of what you hope to produce

- ✔ Illustrations or animated panels you want to show onscreen to highlight a film's story

- ✔ Existing video or news clips that relate to your product or eventual goal

- ✔ Music clips or downloads for purchase that fit with the theme of your project

Choosing tools to make a great video

Gone are the days when you needed expensive editing equipment to make a video. Because you're not posting a video for broadcast television, it doesn't need to be HD resolution, although many phones and small cameras can shoot video in HD. Even if you don't actually have video footage for the project, you can use a number of tools to turn still photos into a video with music or other sound. Two major computer-based resources to try are

- ✔ **iMovie:** This drag-and-drop program comes standard on most Mac computers now and allows you to input video clips, photos, and music into a central file and edit them together into a finished piece.

- ✔ **Windows Movie Maker:** Part of the Microsoft suite of software often found on PCs that have recent versions of Windows and Office installed. If it is not pre-installed on your computer, you can download it from the Microsoft website at Microsoft.com.

If you don't have access to a desktop-based editing program or are intimidated by the idea of using one, there are other, extremely user-friendly ways to create a video — even from still photos:

✔ **Animoto** (`http://animoto.com`)**:** This web-based tool enables you to create an unlimited number of 30-second videos for free, using a drag-and-drop tool. You can become a member for as little as $30/year to get access to templates and music to make videos of any duration.

Log on to the website to start your video project, as shown in Figure 2-3.

You then can begin uploading your raw data, such as videos and still photos, as shown in Figure 2-4. You then manipulate your video elements to tell your Kickstarter story.

Music adds an important element to any video project and can create a fun, serious, energetic, or lighthearted mood. Figure 2-5 shows a sample selection of Animoto's musical library. Choose a track and let Animoto match the music to your images.

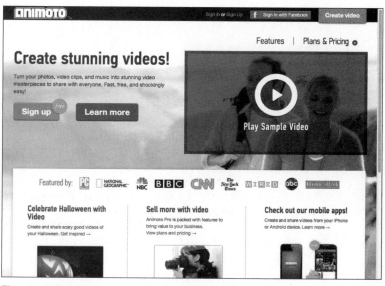

Figure 2-3: Animoto uses easy drag-and-drop technology.

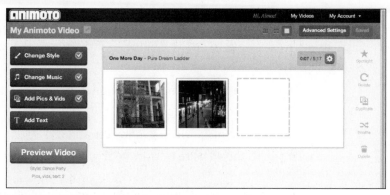

Figure 2-4: Upload a collection of clips and images in any order.

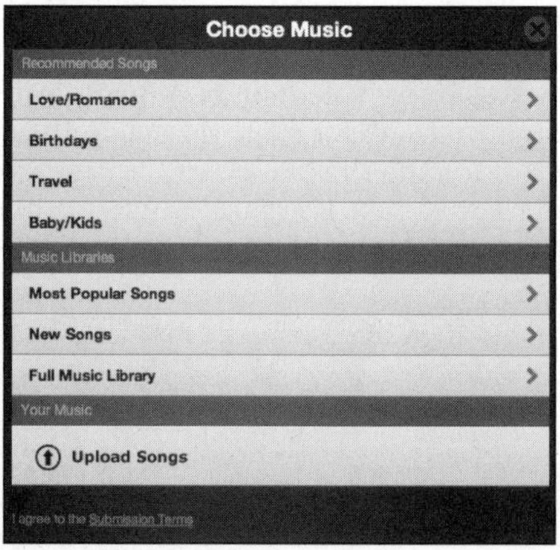

Choose Music

Recommended Songs

Love/Romance ›

Birthdays ›

Travel ›

Baby/Kids ›

Music Libraries

Most Popular Songs ›

New Songs ›

Full Music Library ›

Your Music

⊕ Upload Songs

I agree to the Submission Terms

Figure 2-5: Select a musical track from Animoto's library.

✔ **YouTube Video Editor** (www.youtube.com/editor):
YouTube already is a great place to upload and showcase
your videos; the website also has a good online tool for basic
editing and enhancement. Using this free editor, you can

- Combine video clips.

- Stabilize blurriness.

- Add transitions and music.

- Make precise timing edits.

YouTube Video Editor does not allow you to integrate still photos like Animoto does, but it is a good tool if you already have a collection of video clips and you need to edit it down into two minutes for your Kickstarter Project Video.

Figure 2-6 shows the user interface for YouTube Video Editor.

✔ **Picasa:** Most people think of Picasa as a photography tool, used to organize and upload photos to web albums. However, this tool from Google also has functions that let you make a video from just your still photos, similar to Animoto. If you don't already have Picasa on your computer, you can download it for free from `www.picasa.google.com`. Install it by clicking the program file in your "downloads" folder or opening the file from where you told your computer to save the program.

After you launch the program, it automatically starts scanning your computer for all the pictures and video files on your hard drive and puts them into the Picasa library. From there, you can quickly start building a project around your Kickstarter video.

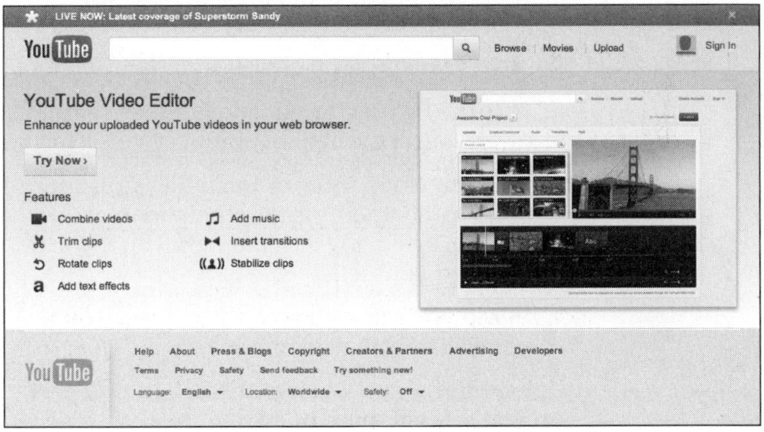

Figure 2-6: YouTube Video Editor helps you export a finished video.

A smartphone is another tool you can use to create a Kickstarter Project Video. Most smartphones (iPhone, Android, BlackBerry, and so on) come with an integrated video camera. For a simple and straightforward video about your project, try the following steps:

1. **Use your phone to film a short two-minute synopsis of the project, showing any relevant visuals, details, or project elements.**

   Remember that you will not be able to edit, manipulate, or change this video; you will have to shoot it in real time, exactly as you would like it to appear online. If you choose this method, you need to have any and all props or visuals already organized and ready, and be sure to monitor your time (to keep it under two minutes). Practice several times before shooting for real.

2. **To save the video to your computer, sync your phone with your computer or e-mail the video file to yourself.**

3. **Preview your video.**

   The following points are good to check, especially if you've filmed the video on a smartphone:

   - Does the video display well on a desktop or laptop as well as on a mobile device?

   - Can you understand the audio throughout the video?

   - Is the lighting bright enough that your potential backers can see what you want the video to show?

   - Is the video jerky or unstable? Consider re-shooting using a tripod, resting the phone on a steady surface, or having a friend help you if you shot the video yourself.

   - Did you remember all the content you planned to include in the video?

4. **Upload the video when you come to that part of your project's development.**

   Chapter 5 walks you through the details of setting up your campaign in Kickstarter.

Understanding Kickstarter Categories

Many people come to the Kickstarter website and browse categories they're already interested in; it's critical to place your project in the category most aligned with your finished product. In the following sections, you find an introduction to each Kickstarter category and tips on choosing the best category for your project.

Introducing the categories

When you first come to the Kickstarter main page, you see a staff pick for the project of the day and a listing of all the Kickstarter categories in a column at the right of the screen. The following list gives you examples of the types of projects that are suitable for each category.

✔ **Art:** The category includes paintings, drawings, sculpture, performance art, digital art, watercolors, pencil art, chalk art, charcoal art, and art schools or instruction. Figure 2-7 shows the Kickstarter campaign page for an art installation at the Dead Sea. The campaign's goal was to highlight the importance of water conservation.

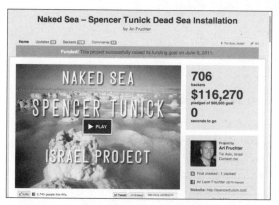

Figure 2-7: This project for an art installation at the Dead Sea was featured in the Art category.

✔ **Comics:** Here you find comic books, ongoing comic strips, online comic series, and products for comic enthusiasts. Figure 2-8 shows the Kickstarter campaign page for *The Bargain,* a graphic novel, which appeared in the Comics category. So did *The Order of the Stick,* a comic strip series that was turned into a printed book. (Find out more about *The Order of the Stick* in Chapter 3.) That project fit this category best because it specifically deals with a comic strip format, even though the campaign was for re-printing of a book-style collection.

✔ **Dance:** Projects in this category include dance recitals, dance troupe costumes, choreography services, and dance festivals. Figure 2-9 is a sample Dance entry, which is a campaign to expand a dance and movement installation into an evening-length dance performance for a festival in Brooklyn.

Figure 2-8: This graphic novel project appeared in the Comics category.

Figure 2-9: This Kickstarter campaign's goal is to expand a modern dance performance.

✔ **Design:** This category is for Kickstarter projects related to product development, modeling/fabrication, and graphic design. Projecteo, shown in Figure 2-10, featured its campaign for a tiny Instagram projector (which enables users to project their Instagram images) in the Design category. Projecteo is a great example of the type of new tool or product that is a good fit for the Design category. See the section, "Choosing the right category," a little later in this chapter for more about deciding whether the Design category is right for your project.

✔ **Fashion:** This category accommodates designers of jewelry and clothing (including hats, scarves, gloves, and accessories). Projects that take the form of fashion shows and product-line launches typically opt for the Fashion category. Figure 2-11 shows a Fashion entry for Iva Jean, which launched a Kickstarter campaign for the creation and distribution of a line of women's clothing that's designed to be clean-cut for work but that also meets the needs of bicycle commuters.

Figure 2-10: The Projecteo campaign appeared in the Design category.

Figure 2-11: Iva Jean is a natural fit for the Fashion category.

✔ **Film & Video:** If your project is a documentary, short film, full-length feature film, instructional video, or web series, it's likely a good fit for the Film & Video category. Figure 2-12 shows a sample Film & Video entry, a campaign for the documentary, *Love Thy Nature,* which explores individual connection with the natural world.

✔ **Food:** Food projects can take various directions, including the launch or development of an edible product, a project for a farmer's market or community co-op, or tools and equipment for chefs or restaurants. Sugar Knife Marshmallows, for example, placed its campaign for a small batch of artisanal marshmallows in the Food category, as shown in Figure 2-13. See "Choosing the right category" later in this chapter if you need help deciding whether your food-related project should appear in Food or in another category, such as Publishing for a cookbook.

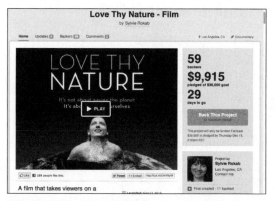

Figure 2-12: *Love Thy Nature* is a documentary and thus appeared in the Film & Video category.

Figure 2-13: Sugar Knife Marshmallows placed its campaign in the Food category.

✔ **Games:** This category covers traditional board games; video games; online games; role-playing games; and equipment such as game accessories, tools, and consoles. Figure 2-14 shows a sample Games entry for a video game called Timber and Stone.

✔ **Music:** If the goal of your project is to fund a musical concert or record an album, the Music category is a good fit. Musicians looking to fund the production costs of creating an album or expanding a short album into a longer project often turn to Kickstarter to raise the funds. One example is Austin Lucas, whose Kickstarter campaign page is shown in Figure 2-15.

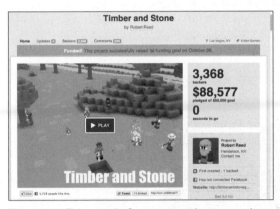

Figure 2-14: This sample Games entry showcases the production of the Timber and Stone video game.

Figure 2-15: Austin Lucas chose the Music category for his campaign to raise funds needed for the production a new studio album.

✔ **Photography:** Shutterbug projects such as photography books, gallery showings, and exhibitions fit the Photography category. Your photo project might be to raise funds for prints, the exhibition space, or production costs. Figure 2-16 shows a campaign for a photography book that features lesbian, gay, bisexual, and transgender athletes.

✔ **Publishing:** This category covers major traditional areas of publishing: fiction books, nonfiction books, photo books, short story anthologies, and journalism. Figure 2-17 shows a sample Publishing entry for a fictional series. The Finding 40 Project, featured in a case study in Chapter 6, also appeared in the Publishing category.

Figure 2-16: This campaign raised money for the production of a photography book on lesbian and gay issues.

Figure 2-17: Sample Publishing entry for the production of a fictional series.

✔ **Technology:** High-tech creativity can find a home in hardware, software, gadgets, or accessories for smartphones/computers. Figure 2-18 shows a Technology entry for a new type of small electronics component board for engineers.

✔ **Theater:** This category is for dramatic plays, musical plays, theater camps and workshops, and theater restorations or upgrades. Figure 2-19 shows a sample Theater entry.

Figure 2-18: TinyDuino appeared in the Technology category.

Figure 2-19: Sample Theater entry for a staged reading of *Fresh,* a new musical whose creators hope to get eventual backers for Broadway.

Choosing the right category

I recommend spending a few minutes on the Kickstarter main page —
before you do anything else — reviewing multiple campaigns in
your likely category.

Possibly your potential campaign could work in more than one category. For example, is a cookbook more appropriate for the Food
category or the Publishing category? To answer this question, I
examine some choices in each category and why they fit one category better than another:

- ✔ **Food:** Most projects in this category have to do specifically
  with the production, distribution, or delivery of food; the
  small batch of artisan marshmallows (refer to Figure 2-13)
  is a natural fit. Are you trying to create a project that has to
  do with eventual distribution of a food product to people (as
  opposed to helping people figure out what to do with that
  food)? Your project belongs in the Food category if it's edible.

- ✔ **Publishing:** Projects in this category would be more closely
  related to the story of — or how-tos related to — food.
  Cookbooks are classic examples. Successful campaigns for
  books about food, such as the *Publishing the +5 of Eating
  Cookbook* and *Trailer Food Diaries: Cookbook*, appear in the
  Publishing/Nonfiction category. That's not to say you can't
  put a cookbook in a Food category. Some authors do, as
  was the case for *Cooking with Fire: The Disaster Cookbook*.
  However, most projects that end up with a finished book
  should be in the Publishing category.

- ✔ **Design:** Many of Kickstarter's most successful campaigns
  come up in the Design category, where clever product designers create innovative new tools or products that customers
  are eager to preorder. In this chapter, I examine the success
  of the Elevation Dock campaign, tapping into one of the largest consumer audiences in the United States: Apple iPhone
  users.

  This product could also fall into two categories: Design or
  Technology. It's important to look at the key central point of
  the campaign: the design and creation of a product that fits
  a market niche or need. This product is not simply another
  gadget or add-on to a phone; it is truly a *design improvement*
  based on others available on the market, hence the placement
  in the Design category.

iPhone Elevation Dock: Realizing a Market Niche

The Kickstarter campaign for the Elevation Dock illustrates how you can pinpoint a product's unique angle and create campaign materials around that angle.

For all the worldwide fans Apple has clamoring for its innovative phone and music products, there seems to always be a problem with one key element: the charging stations. Often, after purchasing a basic Apple product, consumers look for ways to *dock* or charge the product that do the job better than the basic plug-in charger issued by the manufacturer. There are many options on the market, but many of those products suffer from a specific design flaw: They don't allow for the protective case.

Consumers who spend hundreds of dollars on a phone or other device often purchase a protective case to shield the item from damage in case of drops or bumps. The problem (and also the opportunity): No one standard size or dimensions can fit all of those products — dozens of models are available for each individual gadget, all made by different companies. A sample aftermarket iPhone case illustrates this point in Figure 2-20:

Figure 2-20: Sample aftermarket case, showing diversity in selection.

Additionally, many of these other aftermarket docks weren't made with the same care and standards as other Apple products have to meet — consumers would complain the docks were too flimsy or lightweight or didn't dock and undock smoothly.

Casey Hopkins of ElevationLab (`http://elevationlab.com`) recognized this challenge in 2011 and began work on a design for the solution — the Elevation Dock, which is specially designed to charge an iPhone regardless of the case size.

A standard Apple Dock sells for $29 and ElevationLab listed its base model for sale on Kickstarter at $59, a price more than 100% higher than that of the manufacturer's version. Why such a difference? According to ElevationLab's website, it's "The Best Dock for iPhone," and the press seemed to agree.

According to a December 2011 writeup in *Wired Magazine* (during the Kickstarter campaign), the Elevation Dock is "the dock Apple should have made." This type of endorsement is extremely powerful for the millions of Apple users who routinely pay a premium to have the latest and best technology. Figure 2-21 shows the manufacturer's version of a dock.

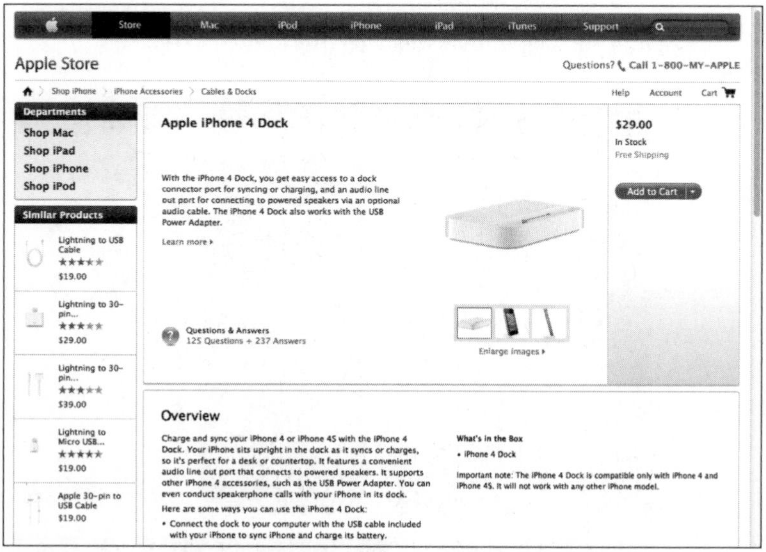

Figure 2-21: Apple's standard dock product.

The Kickstarter campaign also tapped into another touchpoint for Apple users: the chance to preorder something before it goes on sale. Apple users notoriously line up around the block when the newest phone is released; the stores are often packed whenever a new generation iPad comes out or an accessory pack is released. These users love to get the newest thing first, ideally before anyone else can get their hands on it.

Elevation Dock's Kickstarter campaign was essentially a pre-sale for the product before it had even gone into official production. The company's original $75,000 goal was to fund a first production run and pre-sell some of the docks.

Surpassing $1.4 million at the end of its campaign in February 2012, the company had raised more than enough to not only fund an entire production run, but also to offer special limited edition "Kickstarter Exclusive" colors and finishes (as shown in Figure 2-22), as well as reseller packs — pre-selling large numbers of docks to retail resellers around the country.

Clearly, this campaign knew its audience.

Figure 2-22: Kickstarter exclusive colors for Elevation Dock.

Chapter 3

Deciding How Much to Ask For

In This Chapter

▶ Knowing what it's gonna take to make your project a reality

▶ Examining other Kickstarter campaigns

▶ Looking for hidden costs

▶ Estimating average donations

*E*very campaign, no matter how large or small, needs a budget and a *fundraising goal*. This goal should be a figure that represents the amount needed to make your creative project a reality, or at least get it underway.

In this chapter, I discuss the steps needed to realistically estimate your budget and determine the approximate likely donation amounts.

Figuring How Much Your Project Will Cost

The first step in determining your fundraising goal for your Kickstarter campaign is determining the scope of your project:

✔ **Are you trying to raise enough funds to complete an entire project all the way to the end?** If you're seeking backers to complete an entire project, you need a rough estimation of the *complete* campaign, not just a jump-start, before you begin setting up your campaign (as outlined in Chapter 5).

✔ **Is your goal to simply raise enough to launch your project or to take it to the next level?** Think briefly about your entire project as you envision it in its completed form. Would there be a natural set of milestones en route to launching the project? For example, would you need funds to buy some essential equipment? Would money be needed to rent gallery space or studio time? These would be major milestones that the funding must reach before you can move farther along in the project. One or more of these milestones could be a good goal to shoot for when you're raising funds to launch the project.

One of the best tools for estimating a project budget is to use an Excel spreadsheet or other charting/calculation software. Using a software program is recommended over hand-tabulating potential costs for several reasons:

- ✔ A spreadsheet is easier to update and modify.

- ✔ A spreadsheet can calculate totals for your budget line items more accurately.

- ✔ You can share a spreadsheet with potential backers.

- ✔ You can also back up a spreadsheet file for added protection.

This section focuses on estimating expenses for your project. Remember that, if your campaign is successful, Kickstarter will also charge you 5 percent of the money you raise and Amazon will charge you credit card processing fees. When you finalize your overall budget spreadsheet, remember to take these fees into account and make sure they won't leave you short of funds to finish your project and deliver your rewards.

Outlining broad expense categories

You probably already have a rough estimate of the elements needed to complete your project; this may be the result of past experience with similar projects or knowledge of other projects in your industry. Even so, it's important to create a comprehensive, specific budget for your new project to ensure that you're asking for the correct amount.

Start your spreadsheet for tabulating estimated costs with six main categories:

- ✔ Research/Licenses/Permits

- ✔ Equipment to rent (including space)

- ✔ Equipment to buy

- ✔ Staff hours or temporary help

✔ Production

✔ Marketing

As shown in Figure 3-1, the preceding six categories will give you a starting point for dropping in estimated costs and help you think about things you haven't considered yet. The equipment to rent or buy are listed as *hard costs,* meaning you have to spend money to make them part of your project.

Column to list specific expenses

Categories of expenses

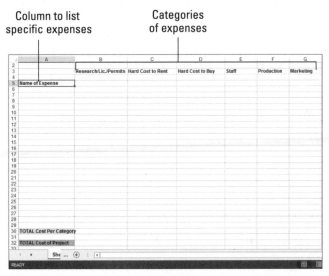

Figure 3-1: A template Excel spreadsheet for estimating costs.

Listing individual expenses

Once you have started a spreadsheet with the six categories, it's time to start listing individual expenses one by one.

Your expenses will differ, depending on the type of project. For example:

✔ For a photography project, you may need to purchase or buy lighting equipment or rent studio time.

✔ For a film, you might have to hire extras or pay an editor to put the rough video together.

✔ For a musical performance, you may need an accompanist or specific instruments to make your vision a reality.

✔ For production of a table lamp, you may have to pay a manufacturing company to produce a plastic prototype or mold.

Your spreadsheet is a good way to start thinking about costs, but you should refer to it several times before finalizing your budget, thinking about things you might have forgotten. For example, you might flesh out your list of expenses as follows:

1. **In your spreadsheet, spend about 20 minutes listing the first things that come to your mind in each category; then put the list away.**

2. **An hour later, reopen the file and look at the list; try to add at least one item to each category.**

3. **The next day, examine your list one last time, attempting to determine what elements you missed the previous two times.**

Figure 3-2 shows a rough-draft Excel spreadsheet with as many potential project expenses as possible for a fictional photographer who wants to make a book.

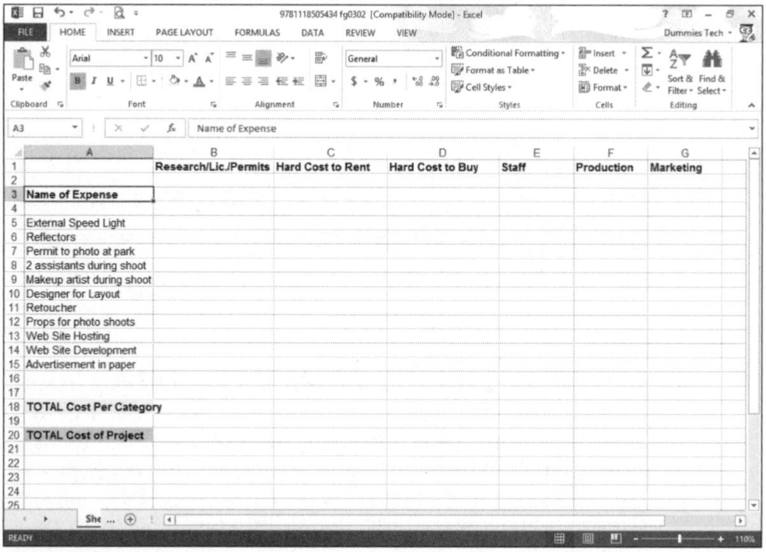

Figure 3-2: Sample spreadsheet with expenses listed but no costs.

Trying to estimate those costs

After creating your list of expenses, it's important to make your estimated cost as accurate as possible. Especially if you've never made a creative project like the one you're interested in launching through Kickstarter, estimating your costs might seem difficult. However, if you've built a spreadsheet as I've described in the preceding sections, you're well on your way. The following sections provide guidelines and ideas for making realistic estimates for each expense category.

Figure 3-3 shows an expanded project-cost spreadsheet with actual costs estimated in and added up.

Name of Expense	Research/Lic./Permits	Hard Cost to Rent	Hard Cost to Buy	Staff	Production	Marketing
External Speed Light			$150.00			
Reflectors			$50.00			
Permit to photo at park	$75.00					
2 assistants during shoot				$232.00		
Makeup artist during shoot				$150.00		
Designer for Layout					$500.00	
Retoucher					$250.00	
Props for photo shoots		$100.00				
Web Site Hosting						$25.00
Web Site Development						$1,000.00
Advertisement in paper						$250.00
TOTAL Cost Per Category	$75.00	$100.00	$200.00	$382.00	$750.00	$1,275.00
TOTAL Cost of Project *(total of all columns)*	$2,782.00					

Figure 3-3: Expanded project spreadsheet with estimated costs.

Research, licenses, and permits

Permits and licenses are typically fixed (hard) costs. To estimate the cost, contact your local, state, or regional agencies, depending on where you plan to work. For research, determine whether you need to pull up old magazine or newspaper articles, access newspaper databases, buy copies of previous recordings, and so on. Then attempt to estimate the costs involved, basing your figure on current pricing listed (usually through the source's website).

Equipment rentals or purchases

For hard costs— such as things you need to buy or rent — try to get as firm a quote as possible. For example:

✔ Call the studio where you want to record and get its current hourly rate. Then estimate how many hours you expect you'll need.

✔ Research camera lighting through Amazon or Google for a ballpark figure.

Be sure to try and get the most accurate pricing possible direct from the source. Do not use Internet chat rooms, blogs, or message boards as your sole source of information for costs; these might be good for estimates, but you will need to check those figures against real-world pricing.

Staff

For hiring extras or basic assistance that does not require education or training, estimate 20 percent above the minimum wage of your state per hour and multiply that by the number of hours you think you will use the help.

Say, for example, you expect you'll need 2 assistants for 2 full-day, 8-hour shoots. And you assume the minimum wage in the U.S. is $7.25 per hour (which is correct as this book goes to press). The calculation for your estimate looks like this:

$$2 \times 16 \times \$7.25 = \$232$$

Your project may require additional skilled staff for part or all of your duration. For example, you might need to hire an additional camera person, a sound technician, editors, makeup artists, and so on. As you estimate these costs for your spreadsheet, the following resources can help:

- ✔ **Job search sites:** Do some basic research on sites such as Craigslist.org or Monster.com to see whether rates are published for positions in these categories.

- ✔ **Industry message boards and websites:** You can also search Google, using phrases such as "average hourly rate for makeup artist" (specify your hometown) to see aggregate amounts on message boards or industry websites.

- ✔ **Quotes from local professionals:** You might want to also place a few phone calls when creating your budget to local skilled staff in your hometown to get their current hourly or daily rates for comparison.

Often these professionals are hired on a daily or half-day rate, so factor in the number of days you might need each type of staff and enter those values in your spreadsheet.

Production

Beyond the costs required to create all your raw materials, you may have an additional "production" cost, or a cost to put your project together in its finished format. This could mean using software to run video clips together, printing a finished book, producing CDs/DVDs, mass-producing your actual finished product (if in the design category), and so forth.

This part of the budgeting process can be the most complicated and often under-estimated. This is a good point to stop and look at your overall Kickstarter campaign and again ask yourself, *Am I seeking backers to just launch me on my way, or am I seeking funding for the entire project from beginning to end?* If the answer is the latter (funding for the whole project), you need to have a realistic budget item for production.

Production is categorized as everything that is not a hard line item (that is, fixed cost) as listed earlier; it's *not* hiring staff, securing location permits, paying for props or designers. It's that nebulous "finishing" step that takes the project from a raw product to a ready-for-delivery product or a prototype to a production model.

Since each Kickstarter project is different, there is no hard-and-fast rule for estimating your production cost. You will need to estimate based on your actual project. The best way to do this is to actually get estimates *in advance* — during this budgeting process — and *not* to wait until after all your raw materials have been gathered or produced.

Some examples of trying to estimate production costs include the following:

- ✔ Getting a firm manufacturing quote from at least three different suppliers if your design product requires mass production.

- ✔ Researching the cost of hiring a software expert or editing expert for the finished product; give this person a production overview and outline of the finished product (how many minutes, how many songs, and other such details that affect the amount of consulting time) and get a firm quote.

- ✔ Get at least three printing quotes — from different types of printers — if you're making a book, comic or magazine; give the printing company as specific a set of requirements as possible, including number of pages, color requirements, cover type, and quantities.

Marketing

Your campaign budget needs to include dollars to promote your end result. After you complete a successful Kickstarter campaign and make the finished creative piece, you need to get out there and sell it!

Marketing and promotion is an extremely broad expense — in some cases, the sky is the limit. But start with the basics. At the very minimum, you should include the following costs in your project budget:

- ✔ Creating and maintaining a website

- ✔ Hosting a launch party, or a viewing or screening event

- ✔ Mailing samples of your product to reporters, writers, and bloggers

- ✔ Participating in fairs/festivals that showcase creative work

- ✔ Advertising (if relevant)

If the audience for a specific publication, website, or news source would be interested in your finished piece, research their advertising costs in advance by requesting a media kit.

In Chapter 6, I examine ways to market and promote your Kickstarter campaign. The details in that chapter can also help you estimate your costs.

Examining other Kickstarter campaigns

So you have entered as many possible expenses as you could think of and estimated their cost. This gave you a project estimate of . . . what? $100? $1,000? $10,000? How do you know if this figure is realistic or completely off the mark?

There's no exact way to know whether your budget is correct, but it's important to examine other campaigns in your category at this point. The following steps walk you through the overall process:

1. **Go to** www.kickstarter.com.

   On the right, you see a list of all 13 possible project categories.

2. **Click the category you think your project will most likely fall under.**

   In Figure 3-4, I clicked Games, which highlighted the staff picks for the Games category in the center of the page.

   Refer to Chapter 2 if you need help deciding what category is best for your project.

3. **Click the option labeled See All (Number) (Category) Projects, as shown in Figure 3-4.**

   For example, See All 281 Games Projects. The number will vary depending on the projects available at any one time.

   All the projects in your category appear, as shown in Figure 3-5.

4. **Spend several minutes clicking through several of the projects in your intended category.**

   Be sure to check out the Staff Picks, Most Popular, Most Funded, and Ending Soon categories within the overall category page. You need to scroll down to see the different ways projects are grouped within the category page, as shown in Figure 3-6.

Figure 3-4: List of Kickstarter project categories.

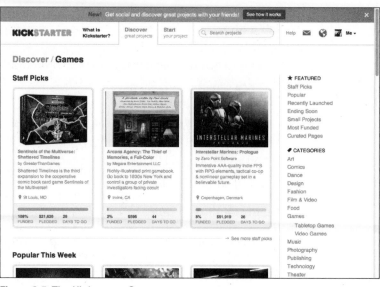

Figure 3-5: The Kickstarter Games category page.

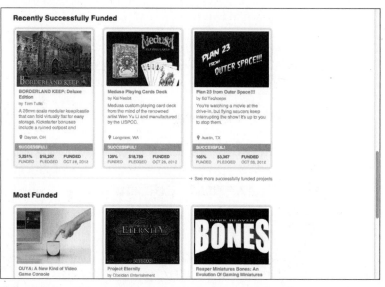

Figure 3-6: Scroll down to see how projects are grouped on the category page.

5. **When you notice a project that's similar to yours, note the funding goal. How much does that project's goal differ from yours?**

   If you see dramatic differences between your potential budget and others in your likely category, it doesn't necessarily mean your budget is wrong, but it may mean you should re-evaluate some of your elements.

6. **Read these project descriptions to see whether a similar project mentions costs that you haven't thought of yet.**

   • **If your estimate is noticeably lower than those of similar projects:** Are you setting yourself up to fall short? Potentially you haven't considered hidden costs, so look thoroughly at these campaigns to see whether something strikes you as a cost you haven't identified.

   • **If your funding goal is substantially higher than those of other projects in your category:** Perhaps you're being overly ambitious in your estimated number of backers or the number of units you might sell or produce. Examine these projects and check how many products they distributed, how many backers they actually received at each level, and so on.

Estimating Potential Donations

When determining your overall project budget, you must also estimate backer pledges.

Kickstarter is an all-or-nothing model, so if you don't get to your project goal, you get none of the pledges.

You can't estimate your pledges as accurately as you can estimate your project costs. But you can make a well-informed guess by following this overall process:

1. **Make a very basic list of people you could consider, off the top of your head, as potential backers.**

2. **Use your project's cost estimate to evaluate how many backers you'd need at different levels. Evaluate whether these levels suit the people on your list of potential backers.**

3. **Consider what rewards might interest your potential backers and the donation amount you could connect to each reward.**

In the sections that follow, you find details and tips for working through each of these steps.

Who you gonna call?

It's not just the signature line from a classic 1980s movie about a team of paranormal hunters. Figuring out who your potential backers are is a key step to Kickstarter success. Like it or not, most of your backers will be people with some personal connection to you, not total strangers. It's time to generate a contact list.

Creating your contact list before you submit your project to Kickstarter for review has several advantages, in addition to helping you estimate your potential donations: Your contact list may spark creative ideas for rewards or changes to your project overview.

The first step in building your potential backer list is looking at all the elements of your life:

- ✔ **Your family:** It's true that blood is thicker than water. Top of your potential solicitation list should be every member of your family, including parents, grandparents, siblings, cousins, second cousins, aunts, uncles, godparents . . . you get the idea!

- ✔ **Your second family:** We often spend more of our days with our co-workers than with actual family members. If you have good social relationships with your co-workers, consider them as a source for your first list of potential backers.

- ✔ **Your community:** Are you active in a religious organization, volunteer group, or other club? You might not think of this group as potential backers, but dozens of potential individuals in these groups would likely want to see your project succeed. You may also have a large online community — separate from a Facebook or Twitter account. Maybe you post actively and have Pinterest boards? Do you post in user groups or message boards? These could also be places to find additional backers.

- ✔ **Your industry:** An important group to consider is the industry in which your project falls. For example, if you want to make a film, your backer list might include film societies, clubs, professional groups, festival organizers, and more. The case study at the end of this chapter (see "The Order of the Stick: Building on a Fan Base and Offering Creative Rewards") looks at an excellent example of a campaign owner working heavily with industry leaders and creating a rallying effect around the project.

Think outside the proverbial box when it comes to ideas to locate potential backers. Look at everyone you come in contact over the course of the week and think about whether they might be interested in your project. Who knows? Your hairstylist might be a secret comic book enthusiast who would love to back your project that creates a new comic superhero who cuts hair in a flash!

Evaluate your potential reward levels

In this step, you experiment with reward levels until you find a comfortable spot for reward levels that your backers might actually fund. Here's how this works:

1. **Divide your estimated project cost by several numbers. Start with 5, 10, 25, 50, 100.**

   Doing this will help you guesstimate the potential number of backers you would need at each level to reach your goal. For example, the total project cost for the film project featured earlier in this chapter is $2,782. Table 3-1 outlines how many backers you'd need at a few basic backer levels:

Table 3-1	Estimating Backers Needed at Different Funding Levels
If All Your Backers Gave	*You'd Need This Many Backers*
$5	557
$10	279
$25	112
$50	56
$100	28

You might also want to consider some backer levels that may be significant to your project. For example, in my campaign for *The Finding 40 Project*, I had (of course) a backer level of $40 for individuals to preorder a copy of the book. If you are working on a film in 2013 and hope to premiere it at a 2014 film festival, a $14 pledge might be a natural fit.

2. **Return to your backer list and consider who might back you at these different amounts.**

   If it becomes obvious that you'll need thousands of backers at a $5 or $10 level — or even a hundred backers at a $50 pledge or more — and if this seems unreasonable to ask of the folks on your target list, consider lowering your overall project goal by 10 to 25 percent and re-calculating before you move on to Step 3.

   To lower your overall project goal without dramatically changing the scope of your project, consider how your Kickstarter campaign might just "kick-start" your project rather than fund it completely. You might want to lower the number of finished copies of your project, limit the scope of what you're producing, or realize that this campaign will only fund the first half of a film or project. Here are some specific ideas:

   - *Use the Kickstarter campaign to create a trailer or teaser* for a feature film instead of the entire finished production.

   - *Produce the first in a series* of comic books, instead of an entire run.

   - *Produce a single prototype* for your design element, realizing that you'll then have to get a loan, attract an investor, or launch another Kickstarter campaign to fund production once you've built a buzz for the product.

3. **If you seem to have enough potential backers to meet your project cost estimate, try working out specific goals for each backer level.**

   For example, if you have a list of 300 potential backers, the $5 donation level is probably too low (because you'd need 557 of them to reach your goal, or 279 — pretty much your whole backer list — to reach even half of your goal). You have a better chance of funding your project if you have a handful of $100 or $50 backers and a larger pool of $25 and $10 backers. Continuing with the film example, you could play with the numbers as shown in Table 3-2.

Table 3-2	Figuring Out Your Specific Backer Goals				
No. of $100 Backers	No. of $50 Backers	No. of $25 Backers	No. of $10 Backers	Total Backers	Total Raised
2	15	75	90	179	$3,725
2	15	60	80	152	$3,000
1	10	50	100	161	$2,850
1	5	50	100	156	$2,600

Using an example like this, you can see the impact even a few larger backers have at reaching your goal and also the combined impact of a few more backers at the lower levels. In the second row of Table 3-2, you see how just adding a few more $50 backers takes you well over your fundraising goal without dramatically increasing your overall number of backers.

Rewarding your backers

Like it or not, almost no one does something for nothing. A very small percentage of your backers will support your campaign without expecting anything in return, but not most. Thankfully, Kickstarter lets you create a series of rewards to say "thank you" to those who back your project and want to see you succeed.

Now that you've built your contact list, determined that your list of contacts could realistically support your fundraising goal, and experimented with the levels of support you need, you're ready to start thinking about possible rewards at each level of support.

Kickstarter allows you to set rewards at any level, from $1 to $10,000 (or more) and to also limit the number of backers at any one level.

The following tips can help you fine-tune the different levels of support for your rewards:

- ✔ **Start with four reward amounts.** You can always add more before your campaign goes live.

- ✔ **Estimate who might contribute at each level.** As a basic guideline, think about the potential backers on your list. How many will be willing and able to give $5? $25? $50? $100?

The likelihood of the number of backers to donate a certain amount will help you determine where to set your levels.

✔ **Make sure one option is a low amount.** Because Kickstarter is a crowdfunding site that's designed to let as many people as possible into your project, you don't want to set your starting reward too high!

After creating a list of your goals for your different backer levels, you need to associate a reward that goes with each amount. Your rewards should correlate to the dollar value invested by the backers, meaning your best rewards should be saved for your largest backers.

Be sure you factor in the cost of your reward when setting the reward level; do not promise a CD to a $10 backer if it costs $15 to produce and deliver each one!

No matter the dollar value, each reward should offer something that has a personal meaning for your backer. These rewards are designed to thank a backer for support of *your* project, not anyone else's. Consequently, rewards should be directly related to the project, not just a random reward. For example, a personal thank-you card showing an image from your project would be ideal.

The following list offers just a few sample ideas of rewards at various levels. I provide a list of other creative backer rewards in Chapter 9:

✔ **$1 – $5 Backers:**

- A thank-you on your project's website

- A personal thank-you card

- The backer's name listed in the finished product

- The backer's name in the credits

✔ **$10 – $25 Backers:**

- Electronic versions of your finished product (e-book, CD/DVD, download)

- Invitations to a performance event

- Invitations to a VIP party for the project

✔ **$25 – $50 Backers:**

- Printed versions of your finished product (book, comic book, photos)

- Finished versions of games, toys

- Signed copies of printed versions

✔ **$100-and-up Backers:**

- Printed thank-yous in project foreword or on the cover or jacket

- Combo packs of e-versions of your project, as well as finished products

- Multiple copies of a project to give as gifts

The list of potential ideas for backers is nearly limitless; if you can think of a creative way to say "thank you," do it!

Figures 3-7, 3-8, and 3-9 show three examples of creative or personalized ways to reward backers: creating a villain, inviting backers to a premiere screening, and cooking a gourmet meal.

Pledge amount	$ 300.00
Reward selection	**Pledge $300 or more** Work with the creators in creating a villain for the next issue, receive a half page ad in the comic, signed print copy, digital cop... view more Estimated delivery: Feb 2013

Figure 3-7: Rewarding backers with the option to create a villain in a comic book.

Premiere screening reward

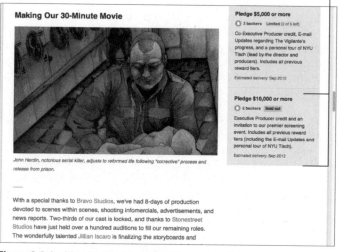

Figure 3-8: Inviting backers to a premiere screening as a reward.

Gourmet meal reward

Figure 3-9: Saying "thank you" by offering to cook your backer a gourmet meal.

The Order of the Stick: Building on a Fan Base and Offering Creative Rewards

Earlier in this chapter, you find out about the importance of assessing your fan base and offering rewards as you figure out your fundraising goal and project budget. In this section, you see how a successful Kickstarter campaign for *The Order of the Stick*, organized by the comic's creator Rich Burlew, used both of these elements.

The Order of the Stick wasn't a new product when it launched on Kickstarter; it had started in 2003 as a once-in-a-while strip on Burlew's personal web page, shown in Figure 3-10. Created as a satirical version of a Dungeons and Dragons type game, this comic features stick-figure style characters competing in a fantasy role-playing scenario. Over time, the comic expanded to several times a week and grew a very large following.

Figure 3-10: *The Order of the Stick* main web page.

In 2005, Burlew began publishing the comic in printed form in basic books. For several years, he published the comic books through his own production house. However, this proved extremely expensive and eventually he found himself unable to continue production, fronting all the costs himself for each run.

From his own posts on his Kickstarter page, Burlew said: "I've been self-publishing my comedy-fantasy-adventure web comic *The Order of the Stick* in paper format since 2005, but one of the hardest parts about doing it all on my own is keeping the older books available. This project is designed to get at least one of those books back into print."

Figure 3-11 shows a sample of a previously printed book.

In January 2012, Burlew launched a Kickstarter campaign to get his books back into production. His goal was $57,750, enough to reprint a select run of books. But as you can see in Figure 3-12, he ended up with more than 20 times his goal, raising $1,254,120. The campaign raised more than enough to reprint the entire series of all the books published up to that point, as well as fund eight new titles to be published over the next year.

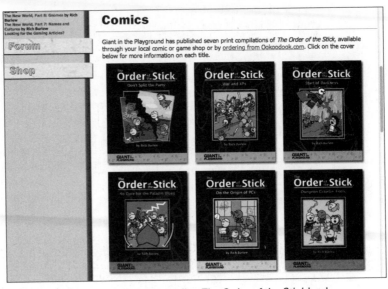

Figure 3-11: Printed version of an earlier *The Order of the Stick* book.

Figure 3-12: Successful Kickstarter campaign page for *The Order of the Stick*.

Building on a fan base

The Order of the Stick had spent several years before the Kickstarter campaign building a fan base. Through publication of the other comic strips and printed books, Burlew had an existing network of thousands of followers through the strip's existing website (www.giantitp.com). This website has a daily average of 150,000 individual page views, giving it a large viewership.

Burlew launched his Kickstarter campaign through his website, communicating directly to his fan base, as shown in Figure 3-13.

Kickstarter campaign announcement

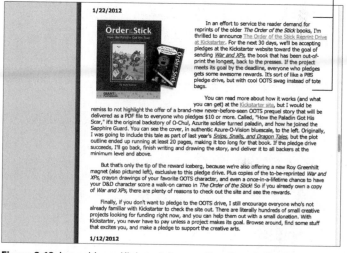

Figure 3-13: Launching a Kickstarter campaign directly through a post on creator's own website.

The Order of the Stick was also already a part of several existing online communities focused on role-playing and web comics — and received exposure for its Kickstarter campaign on ComicsBeat, as shown in Figure 3-14.

As recommended in Chapter 6, Facebook is a great way to communicate with your potential backer group and spread the word about your Kickstarter campaign. Because *Order of the Stick* was an established product with an existing fan base on Facebook, posting heavily on the strip's Facebook page and providing a link to the Kickstarter campaign (as shown in Figure 3-15) was a logical choice.

Figure 3-14: *The Order of the Stick* mentioned on industry website ComicsBeat.

Figure 3-15: Using Facebook in your fan base to launch a Kickstarter campaign.

Chapter 6 goes into detail about spreading the word about your Kickstarter campaign among your communities after your campaign launches. However, it's never too early to begin thinking about who all your potential supporters are — and where you might connect with them.

Getting creative with rewards

Another reason this campaign was so successful was the extreme diversity and variety of pledge levels and backer rewards. It wasn't just a few high-rolling backers giving tens of thousands of dollars to meet this goal; it was thousands of individual smaller backers — which is the true power of crowdfunding.

Here's a small sampling of the more than 50 different reward-and-pledge combinations:

- ✔ $10 (lowest reward available, 2,256 sold): A Roy Greenhilt fridge magnet, exclusive to this pledge drive, shipped anywhere in the world. Plus a digital PDF of the original *Order of the Stick* story, "How the Paladin Got His Scar," when it is completed. (Note: All rewards below this level include the digital download as well.)

- ✔ $26 reward (772 sold): One newly printed copy of *On the Origin of PCs* plus a Roy Greenhilt magnet, shipped anywhere in the United States.

- ✔ $49 reward (74 sold): PATIENCE for a SIGNED PRINT: The 8x10 art print, autographed by the author, plus the Roy Greenhilt magnet and the coloring book and stuff. Add any one signed book for an additional $45.

- ✔ $240 reward (25 sold): A complete set of all 8 limited-edition *Order of the Stick* (OOTS) holiday ornaments from 2004 to 2011, signed by the artist, Rich Burlew, plus a Roy Greenhilt magnet. Add one signed copy of every OOTS book for $262.

- ✔ $675 reward (10 sold): PATIENCE for YOUR D&D PARTY: An original full-color crayon drawing of your D&D party (or party from another RPG, up to 6 characters) based on your descriptions, made and signed by Rich Burlew and shipped anywhere in the world, plus six Roy Greenhilt magnets, six of all the other free stuff, six art prints, six patches, and one copy of the Sticky Shticks expansion.

At the top end of the spectrum, several *Order of the Stick* rewards showcase the possibility of high-end backers pledging large amounts to truly get involved with the project:

With countless characters in the series, one of the rewards was the option to choose a character to feature in a new story; three backers chose this reward as shown on the left in Figure 3-16.

One backer even selected the highest-level reward ($5,000), giving the backer an opportunity to actually create an original *Order of the Stick* character, working directly with the creator, as shown on the right in Figure 3-16.

Story about a character of your choice

Pledge $1,250 or more

3 backers   Sold out

A short OOTS story (8-12 pages) about any character of your choice from the comic strip, delivered as a PDF file to you and everyone else who pledges. Basically, you choose the character you want to learn more about, I write the story, and everyone gets to see it. Plus a crayon drawing of that character, an autographed copy of War and XPs, and the Roy Greenhilt magnet, shipped anywhere. (Note: You may choose any character from any OOTS comic—living, dead, or even unnamed—as long as someone else doesn't own the intellectual property rights to them. Or instead of a character, you may choose a fairy tale or classic public domain novel to receive a StickTales retelling.)

Estimated delivery: Jun 2012

Create an original character

Pledge $5,000 or more

1 backer   Sold out

Your original D&D character, based on your descriptions (within reason), gets a walk-on cameo in The Order of the Stick webcomic sometime this year. Plus, you get an original signed crayon drawing of that character, an autographed copy of War and XPs, and the Roy Greenhilt magnet.

Estimated delivery: Dec 2012

Figure 3-16: (Left) Backers choosing which characters return in the new series as part of the *Order of the Stick* Kickstarter campaign. (Right) This top-level reward featuring the opportunity to create your own character for *The Order of the Stick*.

What makes these rewards so successful? Here are a few key points to take away from *The Order of the Stick's* successful campaign:

- ✔ There were many levels to choose from.
- ✔ Rewards built upon each other, making the jumps in backer levels worthwhile.
- ✔ The rewards were different enough to have something for every type of fan.

> ✔ There was a sense of urgency (some rewards only had very limited availability).
>
> ✔ Many of the rewards were for pledges under $50, allowing a large number of backers to get involved.

Throwing in the perks

Another area where *The Order of the Stick* was successful was throwing in *perks* — added features that served as premiums at various backer levels. What made these add-ons extremely successful is they usually came with an additional backer contribution.

For example, if you chose a backer reward at $25, you could upsell the pledge to $30 in exchange for adding another book to your reward. This incrementally small increase in rewards allowed the campaign creator to increase his overall funding by slightly enhancing the amount each donor pledged.

Figure 3-17 shows a backer perk for raising the pledge by just $5.

Add a book for $5 extra

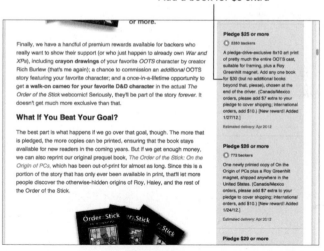

Figure 3-17: Bonus reward for increasing pledge from $25 to $30.

Chapter 4

Creating a Realistic Timeline

● ●

In This Chapter

▶ Estimating delivery dates for your rewards

▶ Timing your rewards just right

▶ Setting deadlines you can meet despite ups and downs

● ●

*O*ne of the largest stumbling blocks Kickstarter users encounter, besides setting a realistic project budget, is the looming deadline: You have to deliver your Kickstarter project on time.

When you set up your campaign (as I explain in Chapter 5), you need to indicate when you expect to deliver your product — and each of your backer rewards. Although, as I write this, Kickstarter does not enforce any regulations requiring campaign owners to deliver finished products or rewards at the times indicated on the campaign's page, you still have to answer to your backers.

In the past few months, there have been several stories in the press and online about frustration with successful Kickstarter campaigns that still have not delivered the promised items. The following two examples of successful Kickstarter projects were either very late with their delivery or still have not delivered at all, resulting in bad press:

✔ **Double Fine Adventure**: This campaign for the creation of a classic "point-and-click adventure" computer game reached its $400,000 goal on the first day. Quickly, word spread and in the end, the campaign raised $3.3 million.

Although this was a great problem to have, the company couldn't cope. Angry backers started posting on the project's Kickstarter page, and reporters started to write about it. In an article on CNNMoney, the campaign creators said, "Originally it was three people working for six months on a bite-sized game." Instead, the company grew to 12 people. As the project's scale grew out of control, the campaign owners could no longer meet their deadlines. Later in this chapter, I talk about how to plan for potential scale-up issues if your campaign is very successful.

The team behind Double Fine Adventure, while needing to spread the word about their project's success to people other than their Kickstarter backers, needed also to stay in very close contact with their backer pool, since these were the people making their project a reality. Figure 4-1 shows a small sample of the 17 updates posted on the campaign's Kickstarter page that were designated "for backers only." Keeping these updates private also helped maintain a sense of community and backers feeling like they were really "in the know" about the project's true status.

✔ **Printrbot:** This cleverly designed all-in-one printer enables users to print their own 3-D plastic pieces for modeling prototypes. The campaign more than beat its goal in early 2012. However, the company was more than three months late in starting the fulfillment process, and some rewards were almost six months late. Some backers became so upset with the delay that the company ended up refunding about $20,000 of the $830,000 raised in the campaign.

Obviously, it's best to avoid bad press (and bad sentiments among your backers) by setting and sticking to the most realistic dates you can — up front. The dates you enter into your campaign page are what set the public's expectations for your project.

Figure 4-1: Backer only updates on Double Fine Adventure's Kickstarter page.

To help you deliver your product — and any rewards that you offer in addition to your product — this chapter helps you to develop a realistic estimated timeline before you launch your campaign.

Creating a Timeline for Your Campaign

Why is it important for you to have a realistic timeline for your project?

- ✔ It gives you a structure to work from.
- ✔ Firm deadlines help ensure forward progress.
- ✔ Backers may feel cheated if you don't deliver on time.
- ✔ Sticking to a timeline and delivering as promised creates a track record of honesty that can help you with any future Kickstarter campaigns.

In this section, I help you determine when your finished product will be available. This process is especially important if you're using Kickstarter to fund complete production of an item or project.

To start, you need the project budget you created, as I discuss in Chapter 3. Ideally, your budget is in a spreadsheet format so you can easily add time estimates next to each item. When you have your budget ready, go through each individual item you've budgeted for and note the estimated number of days, weeks, or months it will take to complete that step. Also, make a note of whether you'll need any resource on a specific date or for a certain timeframe.

If you're already familiar with a project-management tool such as Microsoft Project or have a fairly complex production process with multiple team members and dependencies for deliverables, you might be more comfortable using Project to manage a timeline, either in conjunction with or instead of a spreadsheet. If you are interested in using Microsoft Project, check out *Project 2013 For Dummies* by Cynthia Stackpole Snyder. Or to get a sense for what Project can do, point your browser to Dummies.com for free articles about setting up timelines and other features in Project.

Here are some tips for estimating time and spotting date-dependent items for the different types of items you have in your spreadsheet:

- **Permits and licenses:** Some permits and licenses are easier to obtain than others. Talk to the agency issuing the permit about how long processing of your application or request might take. Don't make an assumption or a guess, even if you think you're making a conservative one.

- **Equipment:** If you're planning to rent equipment, make sure you can rent it for the timeframe in which you have specified. Find out how far in advance to reserve any items you need. Discuss the lender's policy on whether you can keep the equipment a few more days if needed. This is especially important if your production totally depends on having the equipment available. If you have to wait until another renter is done before you can borrow the equipment again, that turn-waiting has the potential to substantially delay your project.

- **Staff:** If you need to coordinate the schedules of several other people, do your best to communicate when those people need to be available for your project and ask them to confirm that they'll be available when you need them. If you need to wait for a key member to return from a trip or fulfill another commitment first, that will have a direct impact on your project timeline and delivery dates. It's wise to talk with potential staff in advance of launching your project to understand what their schedules are and where delays might occur. That way, you can adjust the overall schedule ahead of time instead of midway through your project.

- **Production:** If you're doing the production yourself, try to map out the specific steps in your process as clearly as possible and consider how much time each step takes as well as how much free time you can devote to the production if you're working around another schedule.

If your Kickstarter campaign is in support of producing a physical item for mass distribution, be sure to include production quotes that cover a range of quantities. You may be hoping to produce only 100 copies of your comic book; however, if your campaign is very successful and you have 1,000 or 10,000 or more backers who want a copy of your book, you'll need to produce those just as quickly as you were planning to produce the original 100. When you get a production estimate for something like printing, make sure you get an idea of how long it would take to create more copies than you originally estimated of a product. The case studies of Elevation Dock and Pebble E-Paper Watch, later in this chapter, illustrate how a successful campaign can create timeline problems during production.

✔ **Working around a day job:** It's important to not overpack this timeline, because you'll still need time to take care of everyday business and your day job. Life happens and that's part of the process.

When you're done creating a rough time estimate for each item in your project, the following process can help you create an estimated timeline for the project overall:

1. **Count up the total number of days/weeks/months each part requires.**

   You now have an estimation of the possible total number of days required to complete the elements requested in your Kickstarter campaign.

2. **Note which elements in your project have time constraints.**

   Maybe some parts of the project are only available on certain days. This could be the case if you're working around a specific event, facility restrictions, personal commitments, and so on.

3. **Now, take out a calendar and mark your anticipated launch date of your campaign.**

   This doesn't have to be exact, just a guesstimate to allow you to plan.

4. **Using the anticipated start date, move forward in time with all the days you've added up and take into account days that might be unavailable or dates you need to include in your project.**

   For example, if you're making a film about an athlete competing in a sporting event and want to film him or her in competition, take into account that you'll have to film those days specifically; you can't film those scenes any sooner than the days on which they're happening. You also can't start editing or production until after you have that footage — so even if you've estimated (say) 21 days for editing, those 21 days can't begin until after you've filmed the raw materials.

   Using the calendar to set a start date and a total of anticipated days (as estimated here), you should be able to calculate your estimated delivery date for your finished product.

   The estimated delivery date calculated here is probably too optimistic, no matter what your project. Even so, don't worry — almost everyone underestimates how long it will take to get a project completed! Remember, once you input your delivery dates in your Kickstarter campaign, they cannot be changed. If you successfully fund your campaign and it becomes obvious you will not be able to meet your stated deadlines, you will need to communicate that to backers through updates as soon as possible. Chapter 8 discusses ways to post updates and communicate with your backers about potential delays and other issues.

5. **Take your estimated delivery date and push it out by at least two weeks.**

There's no harm in delivering a finished product early. However, your backers will become disillusioned if they continue to wait and wait and wait for the reward.

Staggering the Reward Dates

One of the beautiful things about Kickstarter is that it allows you to be flexible, setting different delivery dates for different levels of rewards.

Because you're going to be setting up a campaign that allows backers to pledge at varying levels, you can offer different types of rewards, some more complex to deliver than others. Chapter 3 helps you figure out backer levels and rewards; in Chapter 5, you find out how to set up rewards information on your campaign dashboard. This section focuses on estimating the timing for the delivery of your rewards. You can most likely divide your rewards into two categories:

- **Rewards that are tied to your absolute finished product:** These include tickets to a film's screening, copies of a finished design product, printed books, gallery showings, and so on. You can use your estimated delivery date for these types of rewards.

- **Rewards you can deliver without the entire finished project:** These rewards include thank-you cards, credits on a project's website, delivery of photos from a project in process, and so forth.

When you're setting up your rewards (as outlined in Chapter 5), be sure to think about which rewards you can deliver sooner than the finished-product date that you estimated. If you can promise an e-book version of your project before a printed version and the e-book is at a different reward level, make the e-book's delivery date a little sooner. Also be sure to consider whether your rewards require extra time to make. For example, if a reward requires you to make many copies of a handmade thank-you card or personalized piece of art, factor the time required to make those rewards into your delivery dates.

Announcing a series of reward dates — and then delivering on them, leading up to your ultimate product delivery — shows progress and reliability.

Experiencing Success and Then Delays

Both the iPhone Elevation Dock and Pebble E-Paper Watch were extremely successful campaigns that also generated a lot of unhappy backers because of unrealistic production deadlines. For both of these products, the campaign owners failed to take into account the production time required for a large amount of their products.

iPhone Elevation Dock

The iPhone Elevation Dock campaign (which I introduce in Chapter 2) blew its goal out of the water when it concluded in February 2012. However, it took some time for the physical docks to begin shipping. The original Kickstarter campaign promised delivery in April 2012, but the first docks did not begin shipping until August, and the company has experienced several delays with fulfillment and production.

Kickstarter allows you to post multiple updates to everyone — or just your backers — through the Post Update function. (I explain how it works in Chapter 8.) The Elevation Dock team used the Update function to keep everyone posted on the production schedule and also to respond to questions. The 23 updates they've posted to date show production photos and shipping updates as a way to prove to backers that their product is coming.

Backers can post comments on the project page — and if they are unhappy with failure to deliver, they *will* let you know! The Elevation Dock Kickstarter page alone has over 2,400 comments, many from people asking where the product is. As a project creator, you can also post in the comments and update anyone who is reading the comment thread. If you get a complaint in your comment section, be sure to reply to that backer directly — and as quickly as possible; you don't want the same person posting again, maybe in a worse mood, that he or she hasn't heard from you.

If you're exploring a Kickstarter campaign that involves design of and delivery of a physical product, be sure to be realistic about estimated delivery dates. Anticipate delays in your original production timeline and think about backing out your anticipated delivery dates by a month or more if possible.

Pebble E-Paper Watch

The Pebble E-Paper Watch was not only successful, it has been called the most successful Kickstarter campaign — for one simple reason: It beat its original fundraising goal 100 times over.

Some of the most popular campaigns of all time (some listed in this book), might well have beaten their goal 10 times over or doubled their original asking figure. The Pebble E-Paper Watch started with an original campaign goal of $100,000 and ended up raising over $10 million.

The product is fairly simple and not necessarily Earth-shattering. The watch connects to your smartphone using Bluetooth, alerting users to incoming calls and messages with a silent vibration.

The design, shown in Figure 4-2, was simple and clean, attracting both design and tech lovers.

Capitalizing on the apps craze, the E-Paper Watch also offers tools that allow you to turn it into a speed/distance computer for your bike or a remote control for your music library on your smartphone.

Figure 4-2: Design of the Pebble E-Paper Watch.

The product wasn't new; the company had actually worked successfully with venture capitalists to raise hundreds of thousands of dollars in the years prior to the Kickstarter campaign. However, the initial funding proved insufficient to turn the idea into a reality.

When launched in April 2012, Pebble's Kickstarter campaign allowed backers to preorder an E-Paper Watch for $115 (it would retail for $150). Within two hours of its launch, the project had met its original $100,000 goal — and eventually had to end its campaign early due to fears of being unable to deliver the finished product. The Kickstarter campaign closed on May 18, 2012 with 68,928 backers totaling $10,266,844 in pledges.

As with the Elevation Dock, the Pebble E-Paper Watch experienced some shipping and delivery delays due to its overwhelming popularity.

Anticipate this potential problem with your project and have a plan in place to stay in touch with backers or others who preorder. For example, Figure 4-3 shows a page from the Pebble website that shows how the company is providing updates and feedback to customers who pre-ordered through the Kickstarter campaign.

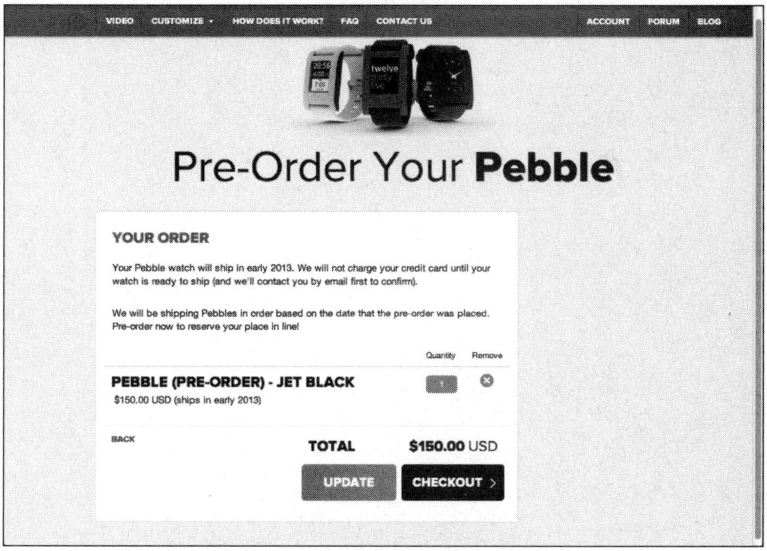

Figure 4-3: Pre-order customer feedback page on Pebble website.

Chapter 5

Setting Up Your Campaign

· ·

In This Chapter

▶ Filling out your project details

▶ Creating your biography

▶ Setting up your payment account

▶ Reviewing your campaign one last time

▶ Submitting your campaign to Kickstarter for approval

· ·

*Y*ou're excited about your project. You know what makes it unique. You've prepared a project description and video with a distinct call to action. Your list of potential backers is ready. You know your project expenses backwards and forwards — and how much money you want to raise. You can't wait to share your creative rewards with your backers.

Does this sound like you? If so, you're definitely ready to set up your campaign in Kickstarter and submit it for review. This chapter walks you through the whole process, from creating your Kickstarter account to reviewing all the details in your Kickstarter dashboard one last time.

 Even if you don't have every detail about your campaign completely nailed down, you might still want to start setting up your campaign. The Kickstarter dashboard is extremely flexible, allowing you to fine-tune your project description and figure out the financial details of your campaign before submitting it for review. Just refer to Chapters 2 and 3 when (for example) you need help with your project profile or rewards, and then return to this chapter for the details about adding these campaign elements into your Kickstarter dashboard. In fact, the verification of your Amazon Payments account and identity can take several days, so you might want to get a head start on those details. I explain how each works in "Activating Your Payment Account," later in this chapter. Kickstarter's approval process will also take at least a full day, maybe two or three, so be sure to factor that in when you're deciding how much time you need to start a project.

After you submit your project for Kickstarter's review and approval, Kickstarter limits the changes you can make to your campaign. This chapter helps you make sure all the details are just right *before* you pass the point where changes aren't allowed.

As I walk you through the process for setting up your campaign, please note the steps and locations of various buttons, tabs, and boxes were correct as this book went to press, but online interfaces can change quickly, subtly, and without notice. So if a step doesn't work quite the way it's described, Kickstarter has likely updated its interface. Nevertheless, the general advice and overall process should still be accurate. You can always check www.dummies.com/go/kickstarterfdupdates for any updates about major changes.

Kickstarting Your Kickstarter Account

Before you can start filling out details about your campaign, you need to set up an account with Kickstarter. Simply follow these steps:

1. **On the top of the main Kickstarter page, locate and click the blue Start link, shown in Figure 5-1.**

   You're taken to a brief video on how Kickstarter works.

Figure 5-1: Starting to set up your Kickstarter account from the home page.

2. **If you haven't already, click Play in the middle of the video screen to review the introductory video.**

3. **After watching the video, click the green Start Your Project button and click Continue to verify that you meet the eligibility requirements for Kickstarter.**

   The requirements are listed on screen and you can find an overview of Kickstarter's requirements and guidelines in Chapter 1. On the resulting page is where you set up your user name and password, or login if you already have a Kickstarter account.

4. **Set up your user name and password or log in using an existing account.**

   You can set up a user name and password unique to Kickstarter or log in with Facebook Connect.

   While setting up your Kickstarter campaign using Facebook Connect might save a few steps, I recommend creating your own unique Kickstarter login and account. You will have the opportunity to link your individual campaign to your Facebook account later, so I recommend linking it there if you choose to use Facebook to promote your campaign. Using Facebook Connect to set up your Kickstarter account means your Facebook account is linked to everything you do on Kickstarter, as opposed to being able to promote and link to a specific campaign. Kickstarter allows you to create multiple campaigns off of one login; you may not want to link every campaign to your Facebook page if you end up doing more than one Kickstarter project.

   - **If you set up a user name and password unique to Kickstarter:** Determine which e-mail address you'd like to use to manage your Kickstarter campaign and a public user name – Ideally your real name so friends, family and associates can search for you even if they don't know the official name of your project. Set up a strong password by using a combination of letters and numbers that's at least eight characters long, doesn't form a natural word (especially not the word *password*), doesn't include numbers in sequence.

   - **If you use Facebook Connect:** Enter the same login information you use for your Facebook account. Kickstarter prompts you to set up a password that's unique to your Kickstarter account.

   When you're done, you move onto the guidelines page.

5. **If you haven't already done so, read the entire Project Guidelines carefully.**

   As I explain in Chapter 1, you want to review the prohibited uses to ensure you don't spend time building a project that will not get approved. For example, fundraising for your favorite charity — or promoting a product that is so outrageous that it will likely never come to fruition — will probably be rejected.

6. **After you acknowledge the Project Guidelines as prompted, click Start Your Project again.**

   Kickstarter directs you to your project dashboard that shows several steps to get your project profile up and running.

   The Guidelines tab on the left gives you quick access to the Kickstarter guidelines at any time. The Preview option the far right enables you to see how your campaign will look to potential backers on the Kickstarter website after your campaign launches.

   Six tabs correlate to the various steps of setting up your campaign in Kickstarter:

   - Basics
   - Rewards
   - Story
   - About You
   - Account
   - Review

The remaining sections in this chapter explain everything you need to know about filling out each tab.

After you set up your account, you can login from the Kickstarter home page. Simply click Log In in the upper-right corner and follow the prompts.

Filling Out Your Project Profile

When you're ready to fill out your project profile on the Basics tab, shown in Figure 5-2, have all the information you developed and fine-tuned in Chapters 2 and 3 handy. Then follow these steps:

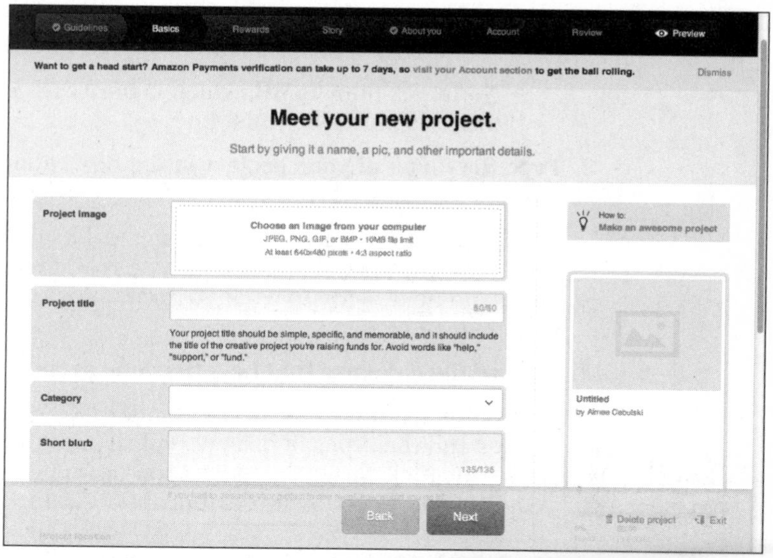

Figure 5-2: You fill out your project profile on the Basics tab of your Kickstarter dashboard.

1. **In the Project Image area, click the Choose an Image from Your Computer link.**

   You're directed to a box where you can select from photos anywhere on your computer.

2. **Browse through your files and select the image you have chosen to represent your project, keeping in mind the 4:3 aspect ratio required by Kickstarter.**

   If necessary, you may have to load different images until you find the one that best fits the 4:3 aspect ratio box Kickstarter uses. In addition, your photo needs to meet the following requirements:

   - **A file format of JPEG, PNG, GIF, or BMP.** The file extension (or three letters after the period in a filename) tells you a file's format. If you have a TIF file (which is another common image format) or a PSD file (which is a proprietary format used in Photoshop and Photoshop Elements), you'll need to convert your image to one of the accepted formats in an image-editing program or ask someone with a little graphics knowledge to help you.

- **At least 640 x 480 pixels,** which ensures your image will appear clearly onscreen and not look pixilated.

- **No larger than 10MB,** which is pretty large, so your image is most likely just fine.

3. **Type the name of your project in the box called Project Title.**

   See Chapter 2 for help choosing a name. Ideally, the name should be relatively short and easy to read in one brief sentence and tie directly to what you're hoping to accomplish with your campaign

4. **Choose the category that best fits your project.**

   In Chapter 2, I introduce all the standard Kickstarter categories and the types of project typical in each. Figure 5-3 shows the Kickstarter Category drop-down menu; move your mouse pointer over the appropriate category and click to select.

5. **Insert your short blurb in the box labeled Short Blurb.**

   In Chapter 2, I discussed the importance of making your blurb concise and compelling in 135 characters or less. In this box, copy and paste the blurb you wrote and character-counted in Word.

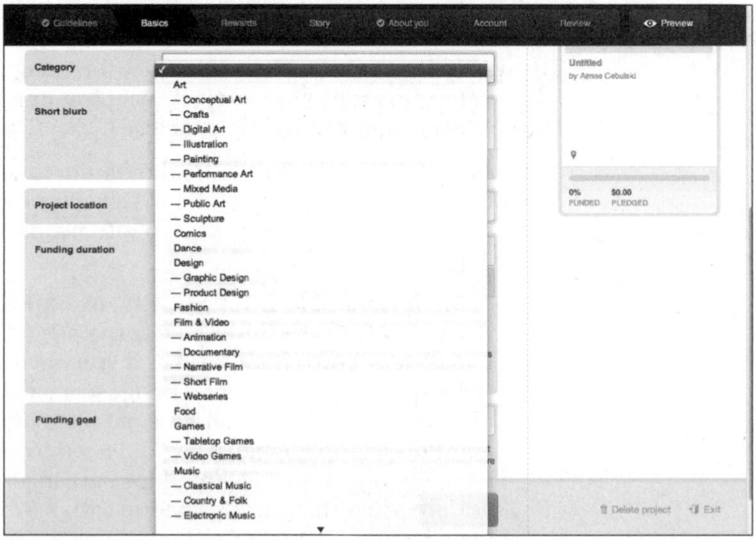

Figure 5-3: Choosing your Kickstarter category from the drop-down menu.

6. **Fill out the Project Location box with your location or the location where the project will take place.**

   For example, if you're shooting a movie on location, place the location here. If you're designing a piece of technology in your home town, type that location.

7. **Type in the number of days for your project in the box labeled Project Duration.**

   A 30–60 day window allows you more time to use public relations, social media, and events to spread the word if appropriate. (There's more about using these tools to promote your campaign later in this book.)

8. **Enter your funding goal as a dollar figure in the box labeled Funding Goal.**

   Figure 5-4 shows where you need to input the goal figure you calculated in Chapter 3. Remember that after you submit your project to Kickstarter, you cannot change this goal. Make sure your zeroes and decimals are all in the right places and that you've accounted for Kickstarter's 5 percent fee as well as Amazon's credit card processing fees. I cover checking all the details of your campaign later in this chapter.

   That's everything you need to include on the Basics tab. Click Preview in the upper-right of your dashboard to see how your entries will look on your Kickstarter campaign page.

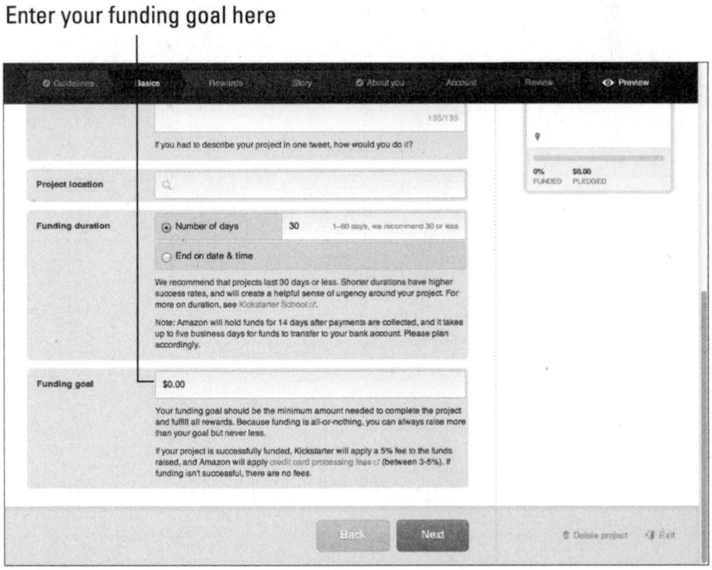

Enter your funding goal here

Figure 5-4: Setting your funding goal.

Setting Up Backer Rewards

Before you fill out the Rewards tab, find your list of backer levels, the reward for each level, and your estimated delivery dates for each reward. (Chapter 3 helps choose rewards and Chapter 4 helps you map out project timelines.)

Then fill out each individual reward box on your Kickstarter dashboard by following these steps:

1. **Click the Rewards tab to begin inputting rewards.**

   You start with a blank box labeled Reward #1, as shown in Figure 5-5.

2. **In the Pledge Amount box, input the dollar amount for your lowest-value reward.**

3. **In the Description box, enter a brief description of the reward that your backers will receive if they support you at the listed dollar amount.**

4. **Select a month and year for your estimated delivery of this reward.**

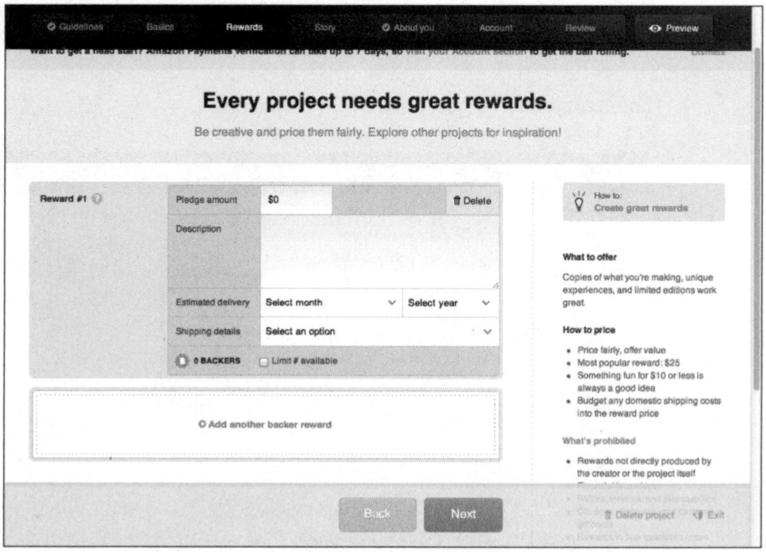

Figure 5-5: Inputting your rewards and dollar amounts into your project.

5. **Select from the following options: Shipping Anywhere in the World, Shipping within the US Only, or No Shipping Involved.**

   If you ship worldwide, you can charge backers outside the U.S. a shipping fee. Simply select the Add a Fee check box and enter an amount. However, you don't have the option to charge U.S. backers a shipping fee, so make sure that fee is included in your cost estimate, as outlined in Chapter 3. Kickstarter recommends you budget domestic shipping into the price of the reward.

6. **When you're ready to enter your next highest reward, click the tile labeled Add Another Backer Reward and repeat Steps 2–6 until you've entered all your rewards.**

   Again, click the Preview button in the upper-left corner to see how your entries will appear on your campaign page.

Telling Your Project's Story

On the Story tab, you upload your campaign video, enter your long project description, and fill out the Risks and Challenges section. Chapter 2 helps you determine what information you need to include in each of these elements.

Uploading your video

When you're ready to upload your video, follow these steps:

1. **Click the Upload Video button.**

2. **Navigate to the video file you previously created and saved on your computer.**

3. **Click the file you want to upload.**

   You see a progress bar as the file uploads; once the file is completely uploaded, a 100% Complete notification lets you know that your video has been successfully uploaded to your project profile.

4. **Click Preview in the upper-right to check your video and make sure you like how it will appear on your campaign page.**

   If you have the option, consider watching the preview on more than one computer to check for possible format issues.

Filling out your project description

If you followed my advice in Chapter 2, you've written and reviewed all the text and images you want to include in your project description already. You can use all the tools of your word-processing software (such as spell checking) to write and review the text. Keep in mind, however, that any formatting you apply in a word processor tool is stripped out of the text when you paste it into the Project Description box in Kickstarter. You also need to use the Kickstarter site's upload tools to insert images, multimedia, and links into your project description.

Here's a list of the Kickstarter text tools and how they work:

- ✔ **Bold:** Select the text you want to apply the bold formatting to and then select the Bold button above the main text box. To remove bold, repeat the same process.

- ✔ **Italic:** Select the text you want to italicize and click the Italic button.

- ✔ **Link:** This tool works in two ways. You can select text you've already entered and click the Link button. The text you selected then points to the URL. Or you can place the text cursor where you want to insert a link, and then click the Link button. The URL that you enter then appears linked in the text area.

- ✔ **Unlink:** This tool removes a link. You can select the whole link or place the text cursor inside the link. Then click the Unlink button to remove the link. The text remains, however, so if you want to remove that, use your keyboard.

- ✔ **List:** This tool applies a bulleted-list treatment. Select the text you want to format as a bulleted list and click the List button. To remove the formatting, select the bulleted text and click the List button again.

- ✔ **Heading:** You can divide your project description into sections by adding headings. Place your heading on its own line and click the Heading tool. Heading text appears larger and bolder so that it stands out from the body text.

To insert multimedia, you have the following tools:

- ✔ **Video:** Adding video at this point is really adding a link to video footage hosted elsewhere; you're not actually uploading video here as you did when you added your Project Video. This option allows you to link to supporting videos about your project or topic, whether or not you created them. If you click

Video here, a pop-up box appears, asking you to paste in a web link from either YouTube or Vimeo.

✔ **Image:** Adding images here is different from using the Video button. If you click Image, you can either upload an image from your computer or enter a website link directly to an image from another web page. If you upload your own image, you're directed to choose the file on your computer; after that file has uploaded, you're prompted to enter an optional caption if you'd like, as well as a click-through link if you would like people to be able to view another website that supports your project.

✔ **Audio:** Adding audio files or links here is very much like using the Image button. You have the option of uploading an audio file from your computer, which must be in MP3, MP4, or WAV format. You can also choose to link to an existing web page here that has audio on it (or an audio-sharing site such as SoundCloud or Rdio).

Adding Details about You

The next tab across the top is called About You, and is designed to give potential backers a little bit of detail about your background and where to connect with you outside of Kickstarter.

✔ **Profile Photo:** This is completely different from any of the images you used in your campaign setup; this photo is just a photo of you as the creative force behind the campaign. Click the box that says "upload an image from your computer" and you're directed to select a photo from your files. Note that the photo's format must be JPEG, PNG, GIF, or BMP and (like your project image) the photo must be at least 640 x 480 pixels to avoid appearing blurry. The photo cannot be larger than 10MB, but again, that is a fairly large size so the clarity of the image will likely not be an issue.

Select a photo that is fairly closely cropped, ideally a head shot or head-and-torso shot; the box showing your photo is fairly small. You want backers to be able to see you clearly.

✔ **Name:** This is where you put your full name, so people can search by your name as well as your project title.

✔ **Facebook Connect:** If you would like to link your personal Facebook page to your project, you can enter the link here; it will take backers directly to that Facebook page if they have valid Facebook accounts.

✔ **Biography:** This should be a short description about you and your experience or background — especially how they relate to this project. If you have an existing résumé, bio, or CV, you have a good place to pull copy. Keep your biography fairly short (400 words or less) and conversational in tone. This description should be easy to read and follow, just as if you were telling someone you just met about your experience.

✔ **Your Location:** Input your current home town here, so that people seeking projects nearby will know you exist.

✔ **Websites:** You can add links here to any external websites that give people a sense of your project or passion. Links to a blog, professional web page, Facebook company or non-personal pages, Twitter feed, Pinterest page, and more are perfect here! You can enter as many websites as you like; just input the URL and click the button that says Add. A new blank box appears above the URL you just added; if you want to, add another website to the list.

Activating Your Payment Account

Kickstarter uses Amazon Payments to process your backer payments.

Click the Account tab to begin the process of activating your Amazon Payments account.

To be eligible to start a Kickstarter project as a U.S. creator, you need to satisfy the requirements of Amazon Payments:

✔ You are a U.S. citizen or a permanent resident with either a Social Security Number or EIN (employer ID number).

✔ You have a U.S. address, U.S. bank account and state-issued ID such as a driver's license.

✔ You have a major U.S. credit or debit card.

✔ You are at least 18 years old.

If you don't meet these criteria, you will not be accepted by Kickstarter. If you do, gather the necessary materials you will need based on the preceding list and then follow these steps:

1. **Click the box labeled Amazon Payments and follow the link.**

2. **If you don't have an Amazon Payments account, you're instructed to set one up.**

   Figure 5-6 shows where on Kickstarter you begin the setup for Amazon Payments.

   Next you verify your identity. This allows Kickstarter to be sure that you are who you say you are.

3. **Click Identity Verification and begin entering the details requested regarding your address, Social Security Number, and driver's license number.**

   The final step in setting up your Account tab is entering your contact details. This is how Kickstarter will contact you with backer updates, questions, or follow-up needs.

4. **Enter your e-mail address and phone number in the boxes where indicated.**

   Be sure that your spam filters are not set too high on whatever e-mail account you use for Kickstarter; otherwise they may reject verification e-mails as spam. You can also set your e-mail spam settings to allow any e-mails from the domain `kickstarter.com`.

   After you've input all the required information in the Account tab, it can take up to 48 hours for everything to be verified.

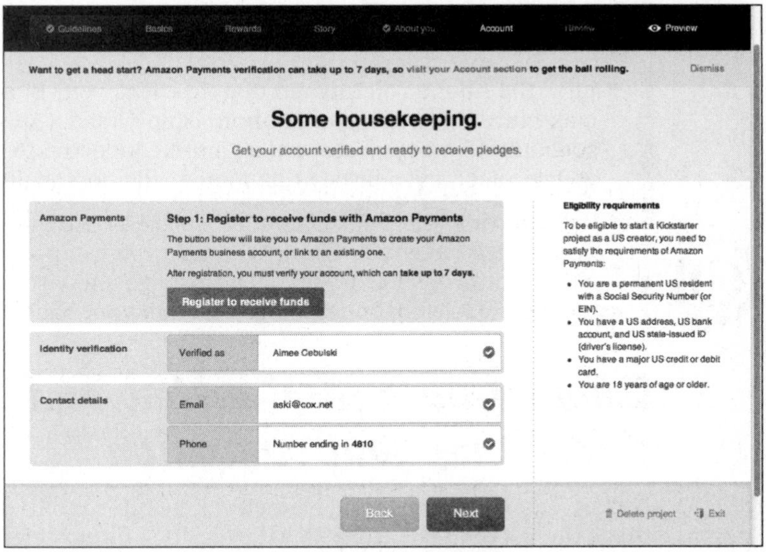

Figure 5-6: Setting up an Amazon Payments account.

Preparing for Kickstarter Review

After all the elements of your campaign have been uploaded into your project page through the Kickstarter dashboard, it's time to submit your project to Kickstarter for review and approval.

It's important to note that not every campaign is approved; some are rejected and need to be modified if they violate the terms, conditions, or other regulations specified by Kickstarter. To ensure that your project is approved quickly, the next section reviews the final steps and checks that you should take before submission.

Double-checking your campaign uploads

Before you move to the Kickstarter Review tab, be sure to check the following:

✔ Take a moment to look at the seven tabs: Are any of them red or do they indicate an X? If so, click that tab and look to see what missing elements Kickstarter is asking for. Correct any errors.

✔ Click the Story tab and make sure that your video has loaded properly: You should see a small thumbnail image from your video. If necessary, re-upload your video until this tab is green.

✔ Click the About You tab and double-check your Biography to make sure that your profile photo is uploaded. (Adding a personal photo makes backers feel more connected to you and your project, even if they don't know you personally.)

✔ If you have a Facebook account, be sure to use the box on this page called Facebook Connect, where you can post updates from your project to your Facebook page and also let people find your Kickstarter campaign through your Facebook page.

Conducting a final review and submitting your campaign

The last tab in the sequence is Review. Click this tab to double-check the list of needs from Kickstarter; look for any elements flagged as red or with an X. The following steps walk you through this tab:

1. **Double-check your funding duration and funding goal one last time.**

   Once your project is accepted, your funding duration and funding goal cannot be changed. You will be able to edit some details of the project and add more photos — even after it has launched — but you won't be able to change your goal or duration.

2. **Click Preview Project to see what your Kickstarter campaign page will look like.**

3. **If you're happy with everything on your dashboard and how your preview looks, click Submit for Review.**

   That's it! Your project will now be reviewed by Kickstarter and will show up as Pending Review when you log in to your account — until you receive an e-mail indicating that the project has been accepted and you're ready to launch. Your project will not be live until it is accepted and you launch it.

Chapter 6

Managing an Active Campaign

In This Chapter

▶ Launching your campaign

▶ Tracking backers

▶ Promoting your deadline

▶ Monitoring fees and costs

*A*fter successfully submitting your project for approval, you should receive notification of acceptance within 48 hours. Congratulations! You're ready to launch your project and watch the backers' support come in — hopefully!

In this chapter I discuss how to officially launch your campaign and start contacting your potential backers. You also find out how to monitor your backers and provide updates throughout the project.

Launching Your Campaign

After you receive approval for your campaign from Kickstarter, your project campaign doesn't automatically go live. You have to launch it. Figure 6-1 shows your project page once you're cleared to launch and go live. (Note the Accepted status that appears in the sidebar on the right.)

Status is Accepted

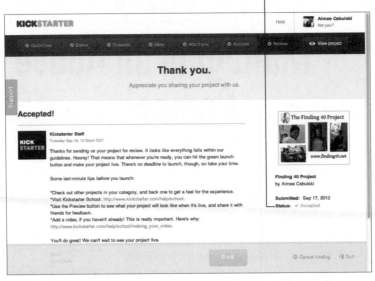

Figure 6-1: Kickstarter project page with status changed to Accepted.

Before you launch your project, you have a chance to review it before your campaign is live and available to potential backers. You can check out the review list in Chapter 5 for general project items to review. Most importantly, this is the last chance to adjust your funding duration and fine-tune the dates for your Kickstarter fundraising window.

Your Kickstarter campaign is *not* live when you get the e-mail message saying your project has been accepted. The e-mail simply means your project is approved to be launched.

Here are some questions to consider before you officially start the clock on your campaign by launching it:

- ✔ **Are you attempting to have your campaign end on a certain milestone date?** If so, look at your duration and count out the number of days to identify your desired ending date and time. Make sure your duration and launch date set you up to meet that milestone end date.

- ✔ **Do you need to avoid overlapping with holidays?** As your fundraising campaign comes to a close, you'll want to promote your deadline to backers and potential backers. (I explain promoting your deadline later in this chapter.) You'll have trouble capturing people's attention during this time if your campaign ends close to Thanksgiving or Christmas, when many people are busy preparing for their holiday celebrations, or if your campaign ends around national holidays, like Memorial Day or the Fourth of July in the U.S., when people often take time off to unplug and be with their friends and families.

If you see that your ending date and any substantial part of your fundraising time overlaps with an important holiday, consider adjusting the start date of your campaign to avoid the potential conflict unless your campaign specifically is related to a major holiday where people might naturally be searching for things around that topic.

✔ **Are you timing your event to coincide with a major industry event or festival?** This could be a worthwhile option if you think there would be a large potential audience for your project and you're planning on attending that event or industry gathering. For example, if you're using Kickstarter to fund a cool new app in the Technology category, and you're attending the SXSW conference in Austin, you might want to make sure your campaign is live during that timeframe and at least a week after, so that you can alert anyone you meet to the opportunity to back your project. On the flip side, if you're not attending or participating in a big industry event, it might be wise to avoid your campaign being live during those dates, because everyone else might be busy with the event. For example, if you're publishing a small comic book series and you're not attending Comic-Con in San Diego, you could face difficulty getting attention of bloggers, writers, and industry leaders during those dates, because they will be covering the industry's largest annual event.

Determine what date you want your project to go live based on your funding duration. If the ending date looks acceptable, you can launch that same day. If not, consider waiting so the end date coincides with a milestone date you have in mind.

After your project is approved, *you cannot change the funding duration*. However, just because you receive notification that your project is approved, you do not have to launch it that day; you can wait.

You will receive an e-mail from Kickstarter that alerts you to the fact that you're ready to launch. To actually launch your campaign, click the link sent in your acceptance e-mail message which will take you to your project dashboard. There, you will see a new green Launch button. Click it to proceed. When your campaign is live, you're ready to start spreading the word.

Creating a Compelling Call to Action

When you make the ask for backers' support, part of your ask needs to include a reason why the project should be completed. Beyond just your desire to make a funny cartoon or entertaining short film, there should be a reasoning behind your project.

Before you begin reaching out to backers, use the following process to create your compelling call to action:

1. **Write down your responses to the following three questions:**

   • *Why* are you interested in your topic?

   • *What* are you hoping to accomplish or achieve?

   • *Who* would most benefit from your project?

2. **Examine the answers, and combine all three concepts into a single paragraph or even one sentence (if possible!).**

   This is your compelling call to action.

Your call to action should be at the very core of your request to potential backers. In the case of my Kickstarter project, I wanted backers to think about the concepts presented in The Finding 40 Project and encourage them to browse the stories and photos of women worldwide, all facing 40. The call was, "Is age just a number? Hear their stories and find your 40!"

Contacting Potential Backers

After you have created an initial list of all your potential backers (Chapter 3 helps you get started), you need to figure out a way to get in touch with all of them. Obviously, you will likely talk one-on-one about your project to your most personal contacts, such as family or close friends. These people care most about what your project means to you and your hopes for their level of support.

However, there will be a large list of people that need different ways of contact. In the sections that follow, you find tips for promoting your Kickstarter campaign through several vehicles.

Sending personal e-mails

E-mail is the most direct way to communicate with individuals on a one-on-one basis. In order to use this technique, you need several things:

✔ Each person's individual e-mail address.

Ensure that these people will recognize an e-mail from you on name alone — meaning that they know you as a person and not just an e-mail list administrator. For example, if you're publishing a photo book on rescue animals for a volunteer group related to animal welfare, and you want to e-mail members of the group, make sure that the people you're e-mailing know of you as an individual and not just as a generic e-mail address such as info@animalgroup.com.

✔ A concise and direct call to action announcing the program and your request for backing.

The following example e-mail, based on my own Kickstarter campaign, illustrates how you can clearly outline your project, deadlines, and goals:

From: Aimee Cebulski

Subject: Preorder your copy of *The Finding 40 Project* through my Kickstarter campaign

Hello!

I am very excited to announce that my Kickstarter campaign for the production of *The Finding 40 Project* is now up and live! This has been an amazing two year process, where I have been compiling a set of interviews and photos of women all around the world, all turning 40 years old. This book is the culmination of those efforts.

You can visit the campaign page here: http://www. kickstarter.com/projects/920030067/finding-40-project

Through the site, you can back the project and preorder an e-book or printed edition (or both) of the finished product based on your backer level. **You can order only through October 31, so order now!**

This has been an amazing process, and I'm excited to be closing in on the end, finishing up my last interviews at the end of the year and aiming for books to ship in Spring 2013.

As always, thank you so much for your support and encouragement!

Thanks in advance for your consideration,

Aimee

Aimee Cebulski

The Finding 40 Project

www.finding40.net

What was I trying to communicate here?

- ✔ The personal nature of the project
- ✔ My specific goals for delivery of rewards
- ✔ A call to action — preordering the book
- ✔ Using a strong subject line to compel a reader to open the e-mail message
- ✔ Making the process as easy as possible for readers, giving them a live link directly to my Kickstarter campaign

Posting on Facebook

If you're raising funds on Kickstarter, you most likely are a member of Facebook. (If you're not very familiar with Facebook, check out the nearby sidebar.) Most Facebook members are aware of the ways people use Facebook to share day-to-day news and pictures of their family, friends, and pets. But Facebook is equally useful for sharing news and updates about your projects, and that includes promoting your Kickstarter campaign. The trick is, how can you keep your Facebook friends informed without wearing them out with fundraising requests?

Many of the people on your potential backer list might already be your Facebook friends. A post on your personal wall is a good way to share information about your Kickstarter campaign in a quick and efficient manner.

When posting on your personal Facebook page, remember that most of the people reading your News Feed are friends and family, likely excited to help you succeed in your project. It's okay here to add a bit more personal information about why your campaign is important to you. But, similar to the person who posts every single hour about the cute things their kid, dog, or spouse does, you don't want to overdo it. To start, I recommend posting an announcement for the launch of your campaign.

Getting started on Facebook and Twitter

Facebook and Twitter are social networking websites. On Facebook, you can choose whose status updates you'd like the follow, and in Facebook jargon, choosing to follow someone's updates is called "adding a friend." Your Facebook friends also see your status updates. Depending on your Facebook privacy settings, only your friends or friends of friends can see your status updates. Facebook does offer the option to make all or some of your posts public, too. To get started on Facebook, visit www.facebook.com and follow the prompts to set up an account. Check out *Facebook For Dummies* or search for Facebook tips at www.dummies.com if you need more help getting started.

Twitter is different from Facebook in two ways: posts (or tweets, as they're often called) are typically public and they're limited to 140 characters. By public, I mean that people can see your tweets whether or not they've joined Twitter and elected to follow you. Anyone following you on Twitter sees your posts in his or her feed. However, anyone you choose to follow on Twitter doesn't see your tweets unless he or she chooses to follow you back. You can set up an account and start exploring how Twitter works at www.twitter.com. If you need more help wrapping your mind around the way Twitter works, check out *Twitter For Dummies* or simply check out the Twitter articles at www.dummies.com.

Figures 6-2 and 6-3 show examples of two different Facebook posts announcing a Kickstarter campaign.

Kickstarter announcement on Facebook

Figure 6-2: Sample Facebook post introducing a Kickstarter campaign.

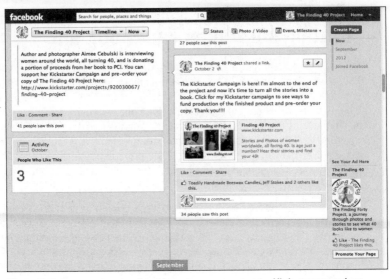

Figure 6-3: A second example of how to announce your Kickstarter project.

After launching the campaign via your Facebook page, it's important to do regular updates that relate to both your requests for support and your generic project updates. One option is to post photos individually from your Kickstarter campaign with a link back to your Kickstarter page. Take a photo you might have used in your long description (embedded using the media tool on your page), post the photo on your Facebook page, and write a short description about what that photo represents. Is it an example of your project in action or something you hope to accomplish? A quick blurb with a link to the Kickstarter page is a way to keep your project top-of-mind for your Facebook network without having to ask directly every single time.

It's important to remember that your Kickstarter campaign is only a small part of your overall Facebook community; you likely have many friends, colleagues and family members in your network. You talk with these people about countless things throughout the day, so make sure you don't turn your Facebook wall into a never-ending sea of posts about your campaign; intersperse your campaign updates with your typical status updates about other topics.

Facebook is a good way to alert people about the countdown to the end of your campaign. Remember to think about the dates on which you might want to post a "few days left" reminder — and work backward from there if you're doing posts every three or four days.

Using a Facebook business page

Beyond having a personal Facebook profile, you also have the option of creating a business page that can be used to promote your project. Similar to a personal page, you, as the administrator, can post updates, photos, links, videos, and more.

This type of page is very different from your personal Facebook profile. Unlike a personal profile, people "like" your page instead of becoming your friend. This way, users elect to see all the information you post on your page in their News Feeds, but you cannot see their personal information.

You can begin the process of starting a Facebook page specifically for your project (if you haven't done so already), by clicking the www.facebook.com/pages/create.php link. From there, you can choose from a list of types of pages:

- ✔ Local Business
- ✔ Company, Organization, or Institution
- ✔ Brand or Product
- ✔ Artist, Band, or Public Figure
- ✔ Entertainment
- ✔ Cause or Community

Based on the nature of your project, select the appropriate category and begin developing your page. You can review *Facebook Marketing For Dummies*, 3rd Edition, by John Haydon, Paul Dunay, and Richard Krueger for additional information on how to build, design, and market your page. A project-specific Facebook page is an excellent additional resource for promoting your Kickstarter campaign.

Begin building your Facebook page before starting your Kickstarter campaign to give you another opportunity for promotion from the day you launch. I started the Facebook page for The Finding 40 Project about six months before I launched my Kickstarter campaign and placed it in the Company, Organization, or Institution category under Websites and Blogs.

Kickstarter has done an excellent job of integrating well with Facebook, realizing that this social media site is a very powerful tool for encouraging crowdfunding. Throughout the Kickstarter site, you can find ways to link your campaign with Facebook:

✔ On your main campaign home page, a button on the far right provides a link to your personal Facebook profile.

✔ Kickstarter has its own business page at `www.facebook.com/Kickstarter` where you can keep updated on the latest projects and modifications to the Kickstarter page. Click the Like button to add this page to your Facebook News Feed.

✔ If you end up creating a business page for your project, you can link to that page in your long description by adding the full website address in the copy and clicking the Link button in the editing box; then users can visit your Facebook business page and potentially "like" it.

Tweeting about your campaign

Although Twitter gives you only 140 characters, you should be able to compel your followers to at least click through to your Kickstarter campaign link to learn more about your project.

Twitter differs from Facebook in one key area: Someone does not have to be your "friend" or "like" your page to see your Twitter post. Once you've posted something to Twitter, it's available for all to search. This can be a great advantage: People who may not be looking for you on Facebook can find your project. But remember to publish only content that you'd want everyone on the Internet to see.

Here are a few tips for creating a Twitter post, or *tweet:*

✔ Keep the content relevant to your campaign.

✔ Use some or part of your Call to Action.

✔ Include a short URL that directs people to your Kickstarter campaign, as shown in Figures 6-4 and 6-5. A short URL is a shortened website address. Using a short URL enables you to include a link your tweet without using up your entire 140-character allotment.

Tweet announcing a Kickstarter campaign

Figure 6-4: A sample Kickstarter announcement on Twitter.

Figure 6-5: These search results for tweets about Kickstarter launches show different ways to announce a Kickstarter launch on Twitter.

Posting your campaign video on video-sharing sites

You've already created a strong project video, so here's another way to use it to your advantage. Since the project video is designed to explain your project in a nutshell, use it to tell your story on other video-sharing sites.

Take the short blurb you already wrote as part of your campaign application and use it as a caption, video title, or description when you upload your video to YouTube and similar video-sharing sites. When you upload a video to a sharing site, you can usually include some information about the video and set a few options. Be sure to follow these tips:

- ✔ **Make your video public.** You want your video to turn up in search results, and you want viewers to have the ability to share the video with their friends.

- ✔ **Add search tags that are associated with the keywords in your description.** Examples include *film, photography,* and so on. Make sure one of these is a keyword relating to the topic of your project.

- ✔ **Include your name.** You want to make sure to develop recognition as the project creator and enable people to find your project via your name if they know you or know of you.

- ✔ **Insert your Kickstarter campaign URL as a clickable link.** For the link to work, you typically need to paste in the full web address with the `http://` in front.

Using your short blurb, keywords, and Kickstarter URL allows users to find you if they search for any of those topics.

Below is a list of some video-sharing sites to consider when posting your project video:

- ✔ YouTube.com
- ✔ Vimeo.com
- ✔ GoogleVideo.com
- ✔ DailyMotion.com
- ✔ Break.com (This one's appropriate if your video is humorous.)
- ✔ FunnyOrDie.com (Again, use this one if your video is humorous.)

Each of the preceding sites has its own requirements for file size, format, upload protocols, and guidelines. Take some time to browse the videos posted on each of these and review the steps required for uploading your Kickstarter campaign video.

Tracking Your Backers

One of Kickstarter's best features is the ability to quickly review how many backers you have, how much money they've pledged, and what reward each has selected. As your project continues, be sure to log in to your Kickstarter account every day and view your current Backer Report and status.

After you launch your project, you can follow these steps to look at your Backer Report at any time:

1. **Go to the main Kickstarter web page and click the Me icon at the top — it should also have your profile picture. Or if you're not logged in, then log in first.**

2. **Click your launched project name.**

   Your project page appears, similar to the one shown in Figure 6-6. Here you see how many backers you have, how much money you've raised, and how much time is left to reach your fundraising goal.

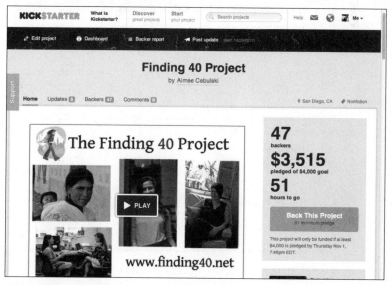

Figure 6-6: A Kickstarter project page looks like this after the project is launched.

At the top of the screen, you see several options — including Edit Project, Dashboard, Backer Report, and Post Update.

3. **Click Backer Report to view your project's backers, as shown in Figure 6-7.**

   At this screen you see a list of the number of backers in each reward category per the guidelines you set up on your project.

4. **To see actual individual backers, click the View Report arrow to the right of each backer level.**

   Figure 6-8 shows a sample Backer Report at the $25 level for a project; notice the individual backers listed, date, and status for each one.

In February 2013, Kickstarter launched an iPhone App available through the App Store. If you have an iPhone, this is a great tool for tracking your backers while you're on the go, as I explain in Chapter 7. If you have a different kind of smartphone, you can probably find a similar app for your mobile operating system. As this book went to press, the only Kickstarter-sponsored app is the iPhone app.

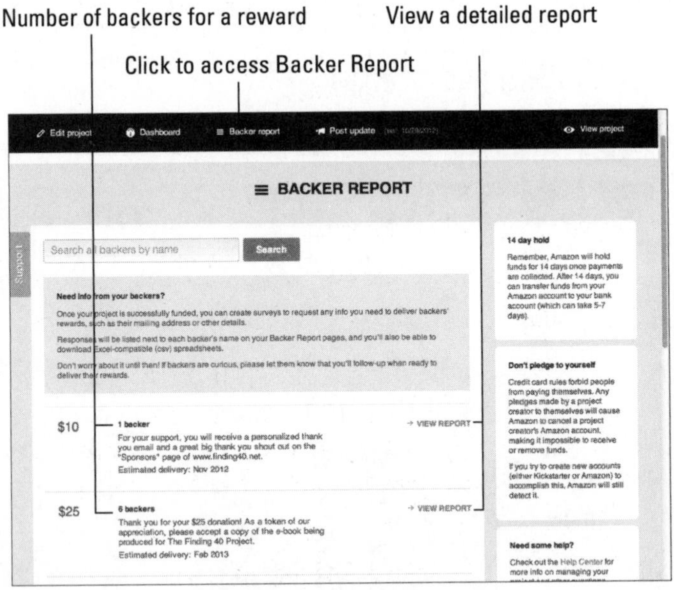

Figure 6-7: The main Backer Report page.

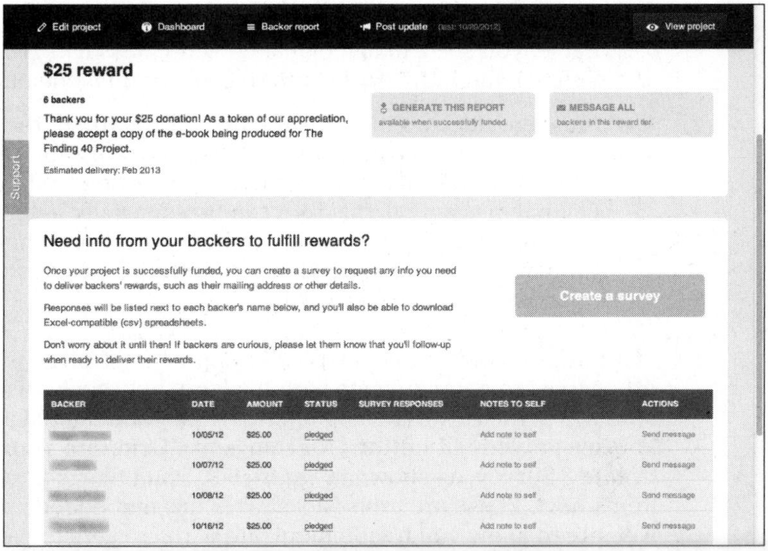

Figure 6-8: The Backer Report for a specific reward level.

Contacting Your Backers through Kickstarter

When you have a Kickstarter campaign, you can use a few different tools on the website to contact your backers. Your options include

- Messaging individual backers.
- Messaging all backers who chose a certain reward.
- Posting an update to all your backers.
- Posting an update to backers that's also visible to anyone who visits your campaign page.

In the following sections, I show you where to find the messaging tools for these options and explain how the tools work.

Sending a message

If you follow the steps in the preceding section to access the Backer Report page for a reward level, you also find two ways to contact your backers (refer to Figure 6-8):

✔ **Message an individual backer:** To the right of each backer's name, you see a mail icon called Send Message. This allows you to send individual notes to backers on a one-on-one basis.

✔ **Message backers in a reward tier:** At the top of the report for a reward level is a Message All link. Click this link to message all backers who share a particular reward tier. While your campaign is active, this tool can be especially helpful if you want to offer perks to backers in a certain tier if they pledge a little more to your campaign. (Chapter 3 explains the concept of adding perks to a reward.)

In addition to messages, the Backer Report page gives you a few other tools to communicate with backers, but those aren't available when you're still raising funds. While your campaign is active, you see grayed-out buttons for things like Generate Your Report or Create a Survey, as shown in Figure 6-9. Don't worry about those items now. These are tools Kickstarter has embedded into the website to allow you to communicate with backers to gather (say) e-mail and mailing addresses for delivery of finished products once your project is complete. Chapter 8 discusses completing your project and communicating with backers in greater depth.

These tools are inactive until your project is funded

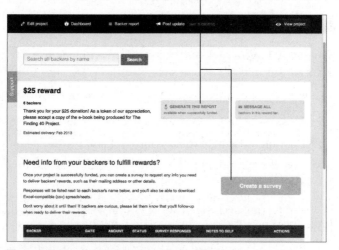

Figure 6-9: Non-active buttons in Backer Report.

Posting updates

Kickstarter has an excellent built-in function that allows you to communicate in bulk to everyone who has already backed your project. You can even use this tool to post generic updates to your project, viewable to everyone, not just to backers. When you post an update, your message and any media that you add appears at the top of your campaign's main page, just above where your video appears. There, people can click Updates and see every public update you've posted to date.

Project updates are a terrific way to

✔ Count down the number of days left. (See "Promoting Your Deadline" later in this chapter for more about this topic.)

✔ Update backers on milestones reached.

✔ Answer questions from backers.

✔ Share photos, videos, or audio relating to your project in action.

To post an update, follow these steps:

1. **On the top of your project page, click the Post Update tab.**

2. **In the Title area, add a title for your update.**

   The title should be short and action-driven, leading with terms that highlight something new or different is happening — such as "Only 3 days left to back the project," or "We've just completed the proofing on our book." These titles should show action, just like a newspaper heading.

3. **In the Body area, enter the text you'd like to appear in your update; use the formatting tools to add bold, italics, links, lists, and so on.**

   The text should also be fairly concise and get quickly to the point about what the update is for. People can read your campaign page for an overview of your project. The update should tell them something that's *not* already on your page.

4. **At the bottom of your Project Update screen, click any of the three Media Upload icons to upload video, audio, or photo files from your computer.**

5. **At the bottom of the Project Update screen, below the Media Upload icons, select who can see your update: Backers Only or Anyone.**

   Make your update public for all to see or just for your backers. Figure 6-10 shows where you select whether an update is public or private.

If your update has sensitive or financial information you only want your committed backers to see, select Backers Only. If you're publishing a more general update and want it viewable by anyone who comes to your Kickstarter page, select Anyone.

6. **Proofread the text of your message to make sure the information is accurate and that you haven't made any spelling or grammar mistakes.**

You can't go back and change an update after you post it, so take your time beforehand, making sure the content of your update is correct.

7. **Click the blue Preview Update button at the bottom of the page to see what your post will look like; check it once again for errors.**

8. **When you've reviewed the Preview, click either Publish or Edit from the two buttons at the top of the screen on the right.**

   • If you need to make changes, click Edit and repeat the editing process.

   • If you're happy with the update, click Publish to make the update go live on your page.

Add media

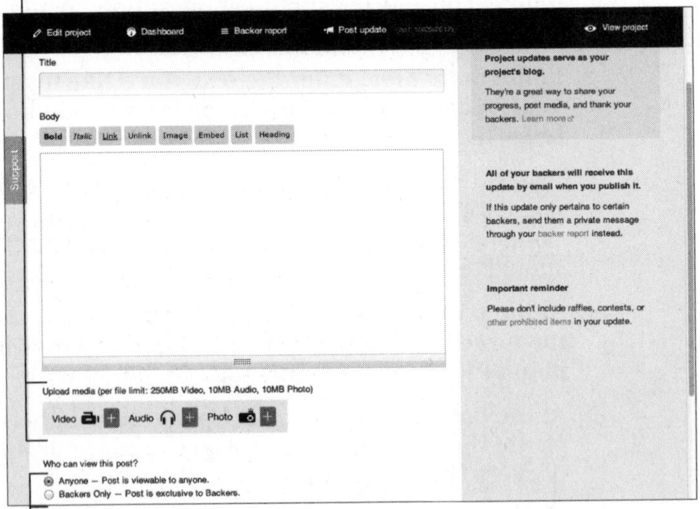

Choose whether update is public or private

Figure 6-10: Choosing public or private viewing options for your updates.

The Kickstarter iPhone app enables you to post updates from the field. It's a great way to post a picture from a video shoot and have it appear in real time, for example. See Chapter 7 for details.

Promoting Your Deadline

All Kickstarter campaigns have a definite end date; if you don't hit your fundraising goal, you don't get any of the money pledged by your backers. Accordingly, it's important to alert both your backers and potential backers about the number of days left for two main reasons:

- ✔ Your existing backers may have other friends who would be interested in supporting your project.

- ✔ Potential backers who received your initial campaign launch communication may have forgotten or may not realize the number of days left in your campaign.

To promote your deadline to your existing backers, you can use project updates, as I explain in the preceding section. Figure 6-11 shows a project update I posted for my Kickstarter campaign just two days before it ended. Note that the title highlights the number of days left and amount of money I still needed to raise in order to meet my goal. In the body of my message, I outlined three specific ways backers could help me reach my goal:

- ✔ Share my project with people they know.

- ✔ Increase their pledge and reward.

- ✔ Preorder additional copies of my book.

To promote your deadline to potential backers, you can use all the same tools I cover for announcing your campaign. (See the earlier section, "Contacting Potential Backers," for details.) Your goal is to encourage backers to come on board before your campaign ends.

Figure 6-12 shows a revised version of a Facebook post highlighting the number of days left in a Kickstarter campaign for the game, Spaghetti & Meatballs. The campaign owner has used his personal Facebook page to let people know his campaign has 17 days left. Note how he also outlines the level of support he needs in order to meet his goal. What's great about this post is it shows how very attainable the goal is if many people participate on a small level, highlighting the power of crowdfunding.

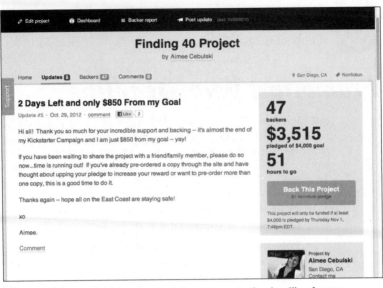

Figure 6-11: I posted this project update to promote the deadline for my Kickstarter campaign.

Post promoting a campaign deadline

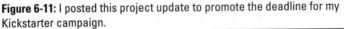

Figure 6-12: This Facebook post highlights the number of days left for the Spaghetti & Meatballs Kickstarter campaign.

You may also have used personal e-mails to introduce your Kickstarter project to family, friends, co-workers, and other contacts. When you have three weeks, two weeks, and one week left, it's a good idea to send a reminder e-mail with the countdown highly emphasized in both the subject line of the message — and visible high up in the content, as shown in Figure 6-13.

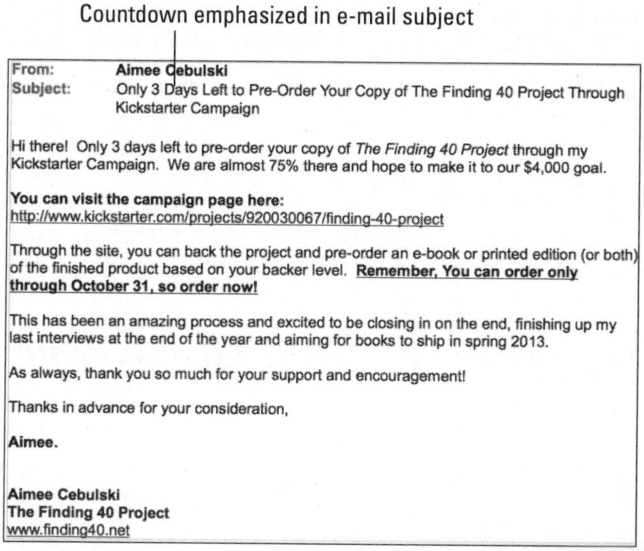

Countdown emphasized in e-mail subject

From: **Aimee Cebulski**
Subject: Only 3 Days Left to Pre-Order Your Copy of The Finding 40 Project Through
             Kickstarter Campaign

Hi there! Only 3 days left to pre-order your copy of *The Finding 40 Project* through my
Kickstarter Campaign. We are almost 75% there and hope to make it to our $4,000 goal.

You can visit the campaign page here:
http://www.kickstarter.com/projects/920030067/finding-40-project

Through the site, you can back the project and pre-order an e-book or printed edition (or both)
of the finished product based on your backer level. **Remember, You can order only
through October 31, so order now!**

This has been an amazing process and excited to be closing in on the end, finishing up my
last interviews at the end of the year and aiming for books to ship in spring 2013.

As always, thank you so much for your support and encouragement!

Thanks in advance for your consideration,

Aimee.

Aimee Cebulski
The Finding 40 Project
www.finding40.net

Figure 6-13: Updated e-mail showing urgency in subject line and content.

Each day, you can log in to your Kickstarter project and see the number of days left to go, your total backers, and the percentage of your total goal received.

Kickstarter is all or nothing! If you find yourself with a week to go and a large percentage left to raise, think about contacting new organizations or groups for potential backers and alerting them to your impending deadline.

Paying to Promote Your Campaign

You have an overall project budget (as developed in Chapter 3). Don't forget to track costs you might spend promoting your Kickstarter campaign against that budget.

For example, you might consider any of the following paid services to promote your campaign and deadline:

✔ Buying a Facebook advertisement

✔ Electing to promote your post on Facebook

✔ Buying an Internet advertisement on an industry website

✔ Taking out an advertisement in a local newspaper to promote your deadline

✔ Hosting events or dinners to educate potential backers about your project

All of these are legitimate ways to promote your deadline — but remember: They all cost money. Be sure to enter these costs into your project spreadsheet (outlined in Chapter 3) so you can track what was spent on the overall project.

Buying advertising on Facebook

Facebook ads are a way to reach a large number of Facebook users around the world without needing to draw them to your business page or becoming your friend. Facebook ads appear on the right side of a user's Facebook News Feed every time they log in. There are two main types of advertisements:

✔ **Display ads** include a photo and text much like an ad in a newspaper or magazine.

✔ **Sponsored story ads** appear onscreen like posts on a wall.

One of the best things about potentially advertising your Kickstarter campaign on Facebook is that you can advertise by location, interests, or connections — and you can target just the people who've already "liked" your page. To support a Kickstarter campaign, you can pick only people in your geographic area if you're promoting a regional event or performance, or everyone interested in a certain topic (such as books, magazines, or product design). Figure 6-14 shows how the targeting works.

The cost to advertise on Facebook varies greatly based on the demand for access to a certain audience, meaning the more a group or geographic area is desired, the higher the advertising rate. Facebook uses a bidding system, where you can set a number that you're willing to pay per click (meaning you pay only when someone actually clicks your ad) or per impression (payment based on a total of how many people viewed your advertisement). Facebook uses a closed bidding system, meaning you do not get to see what others pay for their ads.

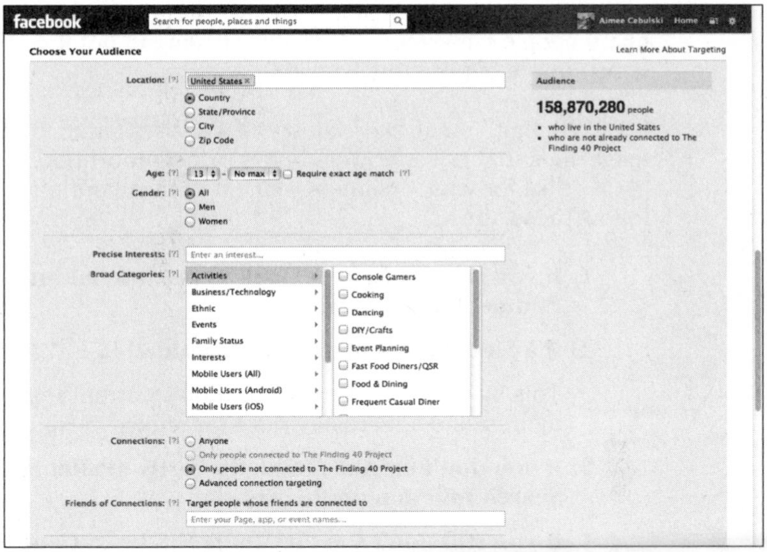

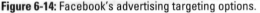

Figure 6-14: Facebook's advertising targeting options.

There is no hard-and-fast way to determine how much a Facebook ad will cost; it could be as low as $100 and as high as $1,000 and up. If you decide to pay for a Facebook advertisement, be sure to put that expense into your master budget as a cost — and look at the number of backers you would have to have (and at what level) to make the benefit to the project worth the cost. When you set up your Facebook advertisement, you determine the budget per day or per lifetime of the ad — meaning that if you reach the target number of clicks or impressions by the end of a certain day, the ad will not run again until the next day, ensuring that you don't go over the budget you've set in your account.

You can learn more about Facebook advertising at www.facebook. com/advertising. This information is correct as this book went to press, but Facebook is constantly changing these tools. For example, just a few months earlier, the promoted post option was not available, and now it is a popular advertising tool on Facebook. Check Facebook's advertising web page for the most current information.

Purchasing other Internet or newspaper ads

Another opportunity for promoting your Kickstarter campaign is a website banner or newspaper ad. This is usually a larger expense than Facebook ads; you may or may not have control over how many people view your actual advertisement, but it could be a good source of potential backers.

It's likely that you already know the websites and newspapers/magazines that cover your industry or neighborhood. In order to get a sense for what an advertisement in these outlets might cost, follow these steps:

1. **If you're on a website, look to see if it has an Advertise or Contact Us tab or button.**

2. **If a Media Kit is available, download it.**

   This kit will have the organization's current reach, audience figures, and advertising rates (as shown in Figure 6-15).

3. **If you don't see the Media Kit easily available, try the Search function on the website.**

4. **If you still don't see the Media Kit, use a Contact button or phone number to request a current Media Kit.**

Figure 6-15: Sample of Media Kit contents.

5. **Review the content provided in the Media Kit.**

   You find options for various sizes and types of advertisements, as well as the minimum run commitments.

6. **Based on the run dates and other specifics of your campaign, request a quote from the ad representative — and then negotiate!**

   Ad rates are always negotiable; it never hurts to ask for a discount.

If you choose to buy an advertisement to promote your Kickstarter campaign, take the timeframe for your campaign into account — and how many times your message will be seen during that 30 or 60 days. Also remember that publications such as magazines and weekly newspapers have a long lead time — the advertising is sold days or weeks in advance. Plan accordingly.

Using promotional events and ideas to drive backers to your campaign

Promotional events are another idea for spreading the word on your Kickstarter campaign. A hosted happy hour is one familiar way to reach out to a group, potentially targeting people you wouldn't reach otherwise. Here are a few ideas for promotional events:

- **Artists' nights:** Look at the restaurants and bars around your home. Do you ever see them hosting artists or displays? Do they have a regular night of the month where local filmmakers come in and show their movies as entertainment for the audience?

  Many local establishments are looking for ways to enhance guests' entertainment without spending additional money. You, as a creative person, might have something to share or add to an establishment's ambiance.

  Figure 6-16 shows a web page for a restaurant called Basic Pizza which hosts local artists on Tuesday evenings. If you're using Kickstarter to create a gallery showing or photo exhibition, this might be a great opportunity to get your work in front of a new audience.

Figure 6-16: Artists' night at Basic Pizza in San Diego.

Spend some time examining opportunities right nearby to participate in an evening like this; you may also want to speak to a manager about potentially hosting your own evening — where you are the only artist present — in exchange for a small fee. Again, such a fee is a hard cost, so be sure to add it to your project budget.

✔ **Raffle events:** This can be an online event tied to your Kickstarter campaign, potentially run via your Facebook or Twitter posts. Post an announcement that everyone who backs your project within the next 24 or 48 hours will be entered into a raffle that will bump them up to the next backer level without an increase in pledge (for example, if you pledge $25 in the designated timeframe, you will get the rewards of a $50 backer for $25).

✔ **Pledge upgrade promotions:** This is an idea for getting your existing backers to up their pledge level. Send a message to everyone that has pledged to a certain level and tell them for a designated time only (24–48 hours), if they increase their pledge to the next level, they will get a premium reward not currently available on the site.

Getting Picky: Project of the Day

When someone first comes to the Kickstarter home page, regardless of location, he or she sees a Project of the Day link to a current project's campaign. If your campaign becomes a Project of the Day, it's a great promotional tool, but unfortunately, you don't have much control over this placement.

There is no specific way to submit your project for consideration as a Project of the Day, but the best ways to make your project stand out include the following:

✔ Create a compelling reason *why* your project needs to happen.

✔ Use an attention-grabbing video that draws people in.

✔ Upload other media, such as photos and audio, that help tell your story and potentially engage the Kickstarter staff to learn more.

I explain the basics of creating compelling content for your campaign in Chapter 2.

iPhone Elevation Dock: Getting the Word Out

Apple fans are often obsessive about getting the latest and best technology — and are picky about what they choose to use with their Apple products. The team at ElevationLab knew this and specifically marketed the Elevation Dock (which I introduce in Chapter 2) as a product worthy of association with the consumer's iPhone.

ElevationLab even crafted its website and images to mimic the look and feel of the main Apple website, as shown in Figure 6-17.

If your Kickstarter campaign is likely to be popular with users of an existing product or service, think of that audience as a potential pool of backers — even if you're not already in touch with them.

So the Elevation Dock was "The Best Dock for your iPhone," according to its campaign creators. How would they let other people know?

A first step was to promote the project within the company's existing client base and friends and families.

Figure 6-17: ElevationLab home page.

To become truly successful and a runaway hit, they needed to reach the Apple fan base — the enthusiastic mass audience that might not even be aware that Kickstarter existed, let alone a product that filled a very real niche.

ElevationLab began blogging, tweeting, and posting on Facebook about the dock and the Kickstarter campaign; bloggers and writers who covered new technology — and Apple in particular — were targeted and sent links to the Kickstarter campaign.

Websites such as TheNextWeb and Gizmodo first picked up and ran with the story that the Elevation Dock was truly better than the Apple-produced product. Once those first hits began to come in, interest in the product began to snowball as stories got tweeted and shared around the tech blogosphere.

Why did the Elevation Dock campaign work so well?

✔ The team included designers trying to create a product that really met a market niche, based on their own personal experience.

✔ The team knew its audience — Apple users — would pay a premium for a better-designed product.

> ✔ The campaign was focused and targeted on a single product with a strong user base.

> ✔ Using the team's own community (tech bloggers) helped to create a buzz.

Finding 40: Learning from My Own Kickstarter Campaign (s)

One of the best ways to become an expert at something is to try, fail, figure out what you did wrong, and try again. Here's where I share my experiences as a Kickstarter user with both a successful and an unsuccessful campaign under my belt. I share my lessons learned about creating compelling content, specifying what the funds are for, and promoting my campaign. When I applied these lessons to my second campaign, I was not only successful, but also doubled my fundraising target.

 You can benefit from my experiences whether you want to review key elements of a successful campaign before you officially launch your project or you're trying to figure out the next steps after an unsuccessful campaign.

Looking at my project

I first became aware of Kickstarter in early 2012 after a friend had used it to fund an art showing. After poking around a bit on the site, I determined this would be a great way to get funding for my book, *The Finding 40 Project* (www.finding40.net).

Since May 2011, I'd been photographing and interviewing women facing the "big 4-0," around the country and internationally. My goal was to create a book of their stories and photos, highlighting what age 40 means, and showing how different it could look.

I thought Kickstarter would be a great way to finish the funding of the project and move me toward a book deal. I needed capital to travel to locations to photograph women — and also to defray the production costs for a proposal.

I began filling out my Kickstarter campaign for *The Finding 40 Project* with details about me, my vision and ambition, and the concept for the book — without really thinking too specifically about my end goal.

Filling the content

Figure 6-18 shows the initial home page for my first campaign.

Here you can see that I'm trying to describe the project and my vision, and to lay out an idea to have the Kickstarter campaign fund the next leg of the project. But I made three key mistakes here:

- ✔ The initial content was too vague and did not grab the reader's attention.
- ✔ The description was too short.
- ✔ I wasn't clear about what I was going to use the money for.

At the time, I thought everyone would be interested in funding my book and following the blog — I didn't even think at all about *why* people should be interested.

Additionally, I failed to use the Project Description section to add any FAQs or other notes.

Kickstarter gives you many opportunities to talk about your project, add a Q&A section, and discuss Risks and Challenges, so use them! The more information you can share about the project, the more potential backers will feel confident about their pledge.

Figure 6-18: The campaign content for my first Kickstarter campaign.

Another key mistake made in my first Kickstarter campaign: I didn't use enough media. I did create and upload a project campaign video, but I didn't add any other supporting photos of the project in action, or women photographed to date. The content page looked very bland, as shown in Figure 6-19.

In Chapter 2, I walk you through tips (and even a few exercises) to help you create good supporting content for your project.

Failing to use my own networks

You can't just expect to put a project up on Kickstarter and expect people to find and back it out of the blue.

I made a classic mistake when I launched my first campaign: I didn't tell anyone about it! Once the campaign went live, I did a single Facebook post and sent one e-mail out to friends and family. As you learn in this chapter, promoting your campaign takes much more than that!

Getting people to pledge to your Kickstarter campaign often involves multiple rounds of contact. You can't just send out one blank message and expect people to all act at once!

The Big 4-0. We think we know what this means, but do we? 40 Women Worldwide , 40 Photos, 40 Stories. Think you know 40? Find out.

Launched: Feb 8, 2012
Funding ended: Mar 9, 2012

Aimee Cebulski 349 friends
Website: finding40.net
See full bio

I'm on a mission -- Finding Forty. As I approach the big 4-0, I know what that milestone means to me, but what does it mean to other women? I am photographing and interviewing 40 different women, all at the same point in life, but all in very different settings around the world. I will tell their stories through photos and narrative, showcasing how different this number can be for women worldwide. *Your support will help me fund the hard costs associated with the next leg of the project, slated for the Middle East and Southern Europe.*

Please enjoy this quick overview of what the Finding 40 Project is all about and some of the wonderful women we have already interviewed along the way...

New videos and updates are always being posted at www.finding40.net.

Thank you so much!

FAQ

Pledge $10 or more
0 backers

You will get a beautiful Finding Forty personal thank you card featuring a photo from one of the locations visited during the project and a thank you listed on www.finding40.net.
Estimated delivery: Mar 2012

Pledge $25 or more
0 backers

For $25, you will get a beautiful Finding Forty personal thank you card featuring a photo from one of the locations visited during the project, with a thank you listed on www.finding40.net with your photo or a logo of your choice.
Estimated delivery: Mar 2012

Pledge $50 or more
0 backers

Figure 6-19: Failing to add enough media creates a bland page.

I also failed to use my larger professional and community networks. I did not reach out to my fellow photographer friends, nor do any PR or blogging.

Not strategizing properly

Here's where the importance of two must-dos crops up: creating a compelling call to action and showing firm reasoning behind your campaign. Your call to action is essential to campaign success. In my first Kickstarter campaign, the call to action was far too vague; backers didn't know what they were really funding.

Even though my fundraising goal was smaller in my first campaign versus my second ($2,000 versus $4,000), I fell far short because backers didn't feel that they understood what the campaign was about.

Instead of using firm words like "printing, production, or design," my first campaign talked about "funding the next leg of the project" and "hard costs," without indicating what those costs were to be.

You're asking backers to help make your project a reality, and they need to know exactly what — in real terms — their money is going toward.

Second campaign: Success!

In October 2012, I launched my second Kickstarter campaign for *The Finding 40 Project*. This time I knew more about what I needed funding for — and how to communicate with backers.

Figure 6-20 shows the revised campaign page, with a much more detailed description and call to action.

This time around, I beat my funding goal and secured $4,281 for production costs. Why did I succeed this time?

- The campaign description was much more specific.
- Backers got a very clear sense of what they were supporting.
- I showed more of the finished product/photos.
- I used media more effectively.
- Backer rewards were tied to finished production elements with firm delivery dates.
- I specifically addressed "Why Kickstarter?" for backers — explaining how traditional publishing had changed.

One of the most important lessons that I learned in the entire process was to *think about what you're trying to accomplish before you even launch your campaign.* If you launch before you have a clear sense of what you need (as I did the first time around), you're likely to fail. If you clarify your goals and do your homework beforehand to figure out what it takes to get there, you've got a shot.

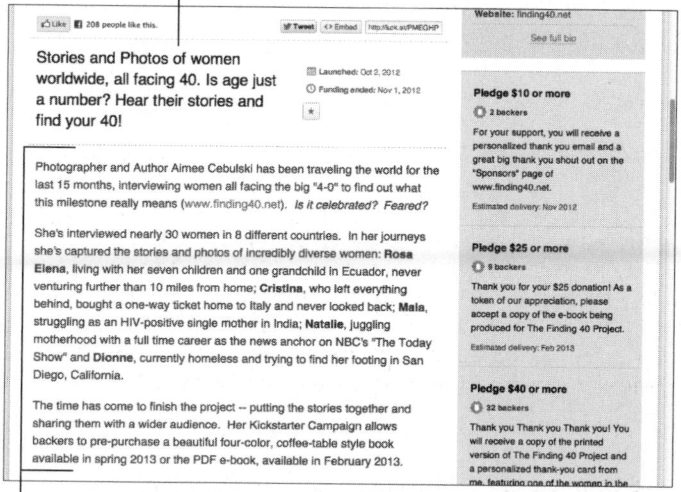

Improved short blurb

More specific and detailed project desription

Figure 6-20: My revised Kickstarter campaign page in October 2012.

Chapter 7

Kickstarter for iPhone

In This Chapter

▶ Downloading the app

▶ Using Kickstarter on your iPhone

*W*e're living in an on-the-go world. Mobile technology is everywhere, and devices like laptops, smartphones, and tablets are not only supplementing but, in some cases, replacing the home computer.

Kickstarter has entered the mobile game with its new Kickstarter app for iPhone.

This new app allows users to manage their account even faster than before. Through the app, campaign owners can:

✔ Find out about new pledges as they happen

✔ Stay better connected with their backer groups

✔ Send photo and video updates right from their iPhones

✔ Search and back countless other Kickstarter projects

The iPhone app is best used to manage, update, and monitor your campaign remotely. Using a laptop or desktop computer is still ideal for setting up a campaign (as I explain in Chapter 5), because these tools enable you to navigate the Kickstarter dashboard and upload media more easily than you can on the app.

As of publication, Kickstarter hasn't sponsored an app for Android, but it might in the near future. If you're an Android user, I recommend checking the Kickstarter site frequently for news and updates. You can also find third-party Kickstarter apps for Android phones. iPad users can use the Kickstarter iPhone app, too, or simply go to the Kickstarter website in the iPad's Safari browser.

Downloading the App

The first step is to download the free Kickstarter app to your iPhone. To do so, follow these steps:

1. **Launch the App Store icon and search for Kickstarter.**

   The app appears on your screen as available for download, as shown in Figure 7-1.

Figure 7-1: Kickstarter app available for download.

2. **Tap the Free button and then tap the Install button, shown in Figure 7-2.**

3. **If prompted, enter your AppleID and password to verify the download.**

   After the app has downloaded, you can tap the Open button in the App Store to open the app immediately. Also, the Kickstarter app icon appears on your Home screen.

   Whenever you want to open the Kickstarter app, simply tap its icon on your Home screen, and the main screen appears, as shown in Figure 7-3.

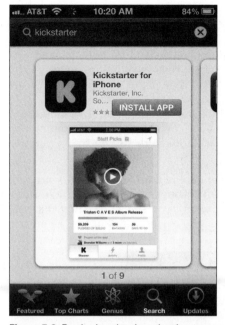

Figure 7-2: Beginning the download process.

Figure 7-3: Main page of the Kickstarter app.

Logging In and Out

To really use the app, you need to first log into your Kickstarter account. If you don't want to stay signed in on your iPhone, you can log out when you're done using the app. Here's how it works:

- ✔ **Log In:** From the main app page, tap Log In in the lower right (refer to Figure 7-3). You then see your existing Kickstarter account, which will look very similar to the screen shown in Figure 7-4.

- ✔ **Log Out:** Tap the Profile icon or the Dashboard icon. From either screen, tap Settings and scroll to the bottom of the Settings screen, where you see a large Log Out button. Tap it and the app asks you to confirm that you want to log out.

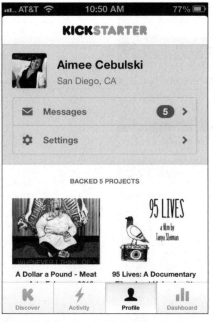

Figure 7-4: Your main Kickstarter app page after you log in.

If you stay logged into the Kickstarter app and your phone is lost or stolen, the app could give anyone access to your Kickstarter account (as well as any other unsecured apps on your iPhone). You wouldn't want to compromise your campaign by giving a stranger the ability to contact your backers as you. (Neither would you want the toddler in your life to contact all your backers accidentally as he or she fiddles with your phone.) Do what you can to keep all the accounts connected to your phone secure and be sure to change all your passwords in the unfortunate event that your phone is lost or stolen. And remember that logging out of the app is a good preventive step to protect access to your campaign.

Touring the Kickstarter App Interface

When you first log in to the app, notice that the default option at the top of the app page is Staff Picks, meaning the staff-picked projects of the day will appear on the main page. Along the bottom are three additional icons: Discover, Activity, and Profile. If you've started setting up your campaign on the Kickstarter website (as I explain in Chapter 5), you also see a Dashboard icon.

By default, the Discover icon is selected, meaning that you're in the part of the app that's designed for discovering Kickstarter projects. The following sections walk you through each area.

Discovering projects

The Discovery area of the app has several areas that enable you to explore Kickstarter projects, just as you'd find on the Kickstarter website. Tap the little green arrow at the top to access the following items, which appear on the screen shown in Figure 7-5:

- **Staff Picks:** You can swipe through a list of staff project picks.

- **Popular:** Scroll through a list of popular projects in this area.

- **Starred:** If you find a project you like, you can give it a star by tapping the project and then tapping the star icon that appears at the lower left.

- **Search:** To search for a project by name, use this search tool. If you have a live Kickstarter campaign, check out how it looks in the app by searching for your campaign by name.

- **Categories:** Below the four tiles at the top, you see a list of Kickstarter project categories. Tap a category to browse projects within that category.

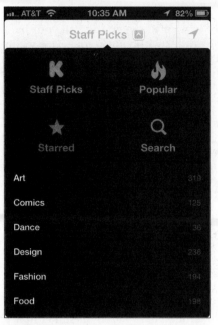

Figure 7-5: A full list of Kickstarter categories.

Checking other projects' activities

The Kickstarter app for iPhone also allows you to follow a friend or back a project. On the main page of the app, you will see a small icon that looks like a lightning bolt labeled Activity. This is separate from the activity of your own Kickstarter campaign that you see in your dashboard.

Tap the Activity icon and you see a list — either of projects you've already backed or of friends' projects you've starred to indicate that you'd like to follow the campaigns' progress.

Tap the name of the project you'd like to look at and you can see the current funds raised towards the project's goal, number of backers, and days left. If the campaign's creator has posted updates, those are visible here as well.

If you've already backed a project, you will see all the available updates. If you have not backed a project and are simply following its progress, you will see only the updates the campaign owner has labeled as Visible to Everyone.

Peeking into your profile

When you tap the icon that says Profile, you will see options for both Messages and Settings.

The Messages function of your profile acts basically like a private e-mail box; these are not public like a Facebook or Twitter posting. You can send and receive messages to individual backers of your project or campaign owners of projects you're interested in. This location is where you will also get messages from the owners of campaigns you've already backed.

These messages are different from the Updates you receive from a backer. If you've backed a campaign and the campaign's owner posts an update for all backers to see, you'll see it as an alert in your Activity page.

Under the Settings icon, you can select how you choose to be updated on various aspects of your Kickstarter account. You will see three different parts of your account: Projects You Back, Creator Notifications, and Social Notifications, as shown in Figure 7-6.

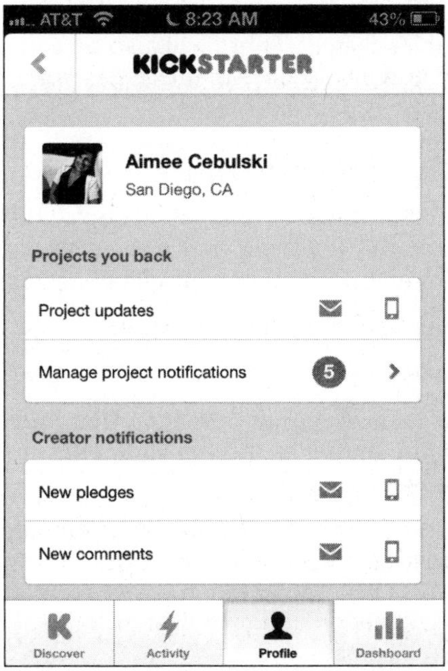

Figure 7-6: Selecting how you receive updates.

Next to each category, you see an icon for an envelope and a mobile device. This allows you to decide whether you would like to be e-mailed about activity and have updates viewable in the mobile app.

The Social Notifications icon allows you to get an alert if one of your friends on Facebook has launched a Kickstarter project; you can then view the project and decide if you would like to back it.

Managing Your Campaign from the Kickstarter App

From this point, you can use the app to view and reply to messages, change your settings, see your account activity, and post updates to your ongoing Kickstarter project. The following sections explain how.

Viewing and replying to messages

When you tap your Dashboard icon, you will see an envelope-looking icon next to the word Messages. There will also be a number just to the right, showing how many unread messages you have. Here's how you view and reply to your messages:

1. **From the Dashboard, tap Messages.**

   The app by default takes you to your inbox, where you can scroll through the previews of any incoming messages (much like a preview pane on your e-mail account).

2. **To open a message, simply tap it once.**

   The full message pops up onscreen.

3. **To reply to this message, tap the icon that looks like a backward-facing arrow in the top-right corner of your screen, as shown in Figure 7-7.**

4. **Type the reply to your sender using the keypad; then, to send your message, tap the arrow at the top-right corner of the green box that looks like a paper airplane.**

   You are returned to the original message and you see the reply below it.

5. **Tap the return-arrow icon at the top-left of the screen to get back to the main part of the Messages functionality.**

Reply

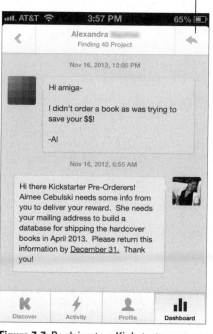

Figure 7-7: Replying to a Kickstarter message.

You can also review any sent messages by simply tapping the small green down-facing arrow just to the right of where it says Inbox. You will see an option to review your sent messages by tapping the paper-airplane icon here.

Seeing your account activity

The Dashboard provides a quick overview of everything going on with your account; you can use the Activity button on your Dashboard to see everything that has happened with your account — including your updates, new backer pledges, and pledge increases from backers — all in a chronological format. The very first item you see when you click Activity is the most recent thing that has happened with your account. This could be a project update you've done for your backers after a successful campaign, a project update for a campaign in progress, the most recent pledge you've received, and so on.

If you're a Facebook user, it's helpful to think of this section as working like the Facebook Timeline model: All the things that have happened in your campaign appear here, in chronological order from newest to oldest.

Posting project updates for your backers

The Kickstarter app is a powerful tool for posting updates about your project. For example, the app can be extremely helpful if you want to do a fast update from the field, such as during a film shoot or product test.

Here's how to post an update with the Kickstarter app:

1. **Tap the icon to launch your Dashboard.**

   You see a large green button right in the middle of the screen that says Post Update.

2. **Tap Post Update to see the screen shown in Figure 7-8.**

Figure 7-8: Posting an update directly from the Kickstarter app.

3. **Using the iPhone keypad, type a title for your update and then type the body of the message you want to send to backers.**

4. **To attach media (such as photos or videos), tap the Attachments button.**

   You see the screen shown in Figure 7-9.

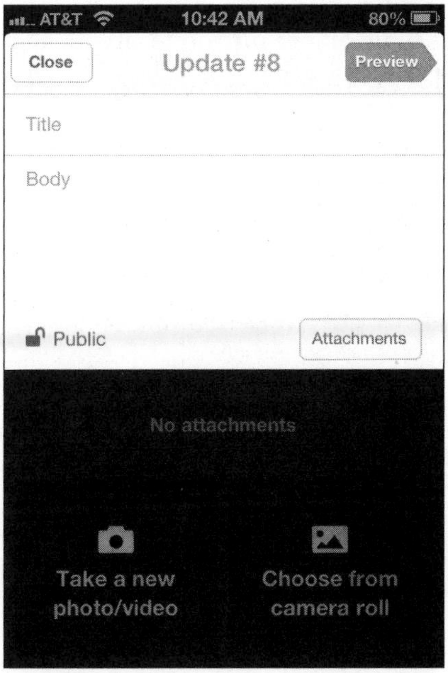

   Figure 7-9: Choosing attachments from your media sources.

5. **Tap either option, depending on what you'd like to do:**
   - Tap Take a New Photo/Video if you want to take new photo or video in real time.
   - Tap Choose from Camera Roll if you want to upload existing media from your camera roll.

6. **Choose whether to make the update public or for backers only.**

   The lower-left corner of this screen shows an open-lock icon that says Public. Leave this alone if you want everyone to be able to see your update. If you want your update only viewable by backers, tap that icon: The icon switches to a closed lock and says Backers Only. You can make the choice — if it's an update that might be of interest to someone considering your project, make it public; if it's something specific or private that you want to share only with people who have already committed to fund your campaign, change the icon to Backers Only.

7. **Tap the Preview green button on the top of this screen to get a look at how your update will appear onscreen.**

    If something seems off or you notice a typo, click Edit on the top left and go back to correct the post and tap Preview again.

8. **When you're satisfied with the update, tap the green Publish button at the top-right of the screen to make your update live on your Kickstarter page.**

Chapter 8

Seeing the Light at the End of Your Campaign

*W*hen you're coming to the end of your campaign, your project may be just beginning. Whether or not your campaign was successful, you can follow up with your backers to ensure they have a positive experience with your project. In this chapter, you find out how the Kickstarter site helps you thank your backers and deliver their rewards. I also help you continue building a community and making the most of your progress so far.

Handling a Struggling or Unsuccessful Campaign

One of the great things about your Kickstarter page is that you'll always know exactly the number of days, hours, and minutes left until your campaign ends. If you've already hit your target goal, this is an exciting time to watch other backers push you up and over the minimum you hoped to raise.

On the other hand, if you're short of your goal, this time can be very trying as you worry about the all-or-nothing aspect of Kickstarter.

If you find yourself below your goal with just a few days (or hours) left, here are some tips that can help you achieve last-minute success with your fundraising:

- ✔ **Be sure to send out time-sensitive e-mails, Facebook posts, Twitter feeds, and more** as outlined in Chapter 6. Remember to highlight exactly how much time is left, make a compelling call to action, and include a link to your fundraising page.

- ✔ **Reach out to your existing backers and ask them to up their pledge to help you reach your target goal.** There's nothing wrong with asking someone in your life (ideally a close friend or relative) to increase his or her pledge (say, by pre-purchasing more copies of a product, buying more tickets to an event, and so on) to ensure that you meet your goal.

- ✔ **Consider looking at your campaign from a new angle:** Is there a group or professional organization you haven't thought of yet? Might there be a group that you're not aware of but that could be interested in your finished product? For example, are you a member of a group with its own specialty media or bloggers? A campaign being directed by a retiree might be of interest to bloggers for groups like the American Association of Retired Persons (AARP), even if the product itself has a wide appeal. A recent campaign led by a paralyzed individual was of interest to disability bloggers because the campaign showcased how Kickstarter can assist creative types who live with a physical disability.

You *cannot* fund your own project; it's against the rules. Kickstarter does not allow you to back a project from your own Amazon Payments account. Do *not* plan on just making up the difference on the very last day.

If you can't raise the funds you need during your campaign, take heart. An unsuccessful campaign isn't a judgment on your idea or your abilities to pursue your passion. You can still make the most of the content you developed and the lessons you learned along the way. Here are ways to follow up on an unsuccessful campaign:

- ✔ First, be sure to thank your backers, as I explain in the upcoming section.

- ✔ Keep an archive of all the materials, notes, and files you used for your campaign; you might be able to use them in another Kickstarter project.

- ✔ In reviewing your lessons learned, make a bulleted list — within two weeks of the campaign's end date — of everything you would do differently next time.

✔ Within four weeks of the campaign's end date, make a list of the successful campaigns within your category that had a similar theme or style; make a point to review those campaigns within the next month and see if you can gather any tips or tidbits from their projects.

✔ On that same list of successful campaigns, consider e-mailing a few campaign owners to ask them what their one biggest trick for success was. Their responses might help spark new ideas.

Thanking Your Backers

Remember, Kickstarter is not just about money — it's about gathering a group of people who believe in your concept or idea. When you come to the end of your project, it's critical to thank your backers, whether you hit your funding goal or not.

To message your backers via your Kickstarter Dashboard, click Backer Report in the top center portion of your screen (within the black bar across the top). You will see an option to send a message to your backers.

Take the time to send each backer an individual e-mail thanking them for their support of your project. This is also an excellent opportunity to encourage an ongoing community with your backers (again, even if you did not meet your funding goal this time).

In your thank-you e-mail, be sure to send backers information on where they can follow your project after this initial phase is over. Send links they can click to get to

✔ Your project's web page

✔ Your Facebook Page

✔ Your Twitter Feed

✔ YouTube or Google Video Channels for the project

✔ A Picasa or Smugmug photo-sharing site

Giving your backers access to this information now allows them not only to follow your project after Kickstarter, but also to interact with each other — further enhancing a sense of community.

Building a Community around Your Project

As is mentioned previously in this chapter, Kickstarter is not just about getting money to fund your idea; it's about gathering together a group of people who all believe in a common goal — in essence, a community. These are people who are also passionate about your idea and are willing to share that passion with others.

In the past, a sense of community meant neighbors coming together and chatting on a street corner or individuals participating in a town hall. In this digital age, a "community" is any opportunity where participants can share ideas and comments freely and collectively.

Sustaining the community after your project ends

Some examples of online community activities include the following:

- ✔ Individuals sharing and forwarding a web page address among friends via e-mail
- ✔ People posting and responding to comments on your Kickstarter project page, as well as on your project's own web page (if applicable)
- ✔ People around the world "liking" your Facebook page
- ✔ Twitter users posting about your project or re-tweeting any of your tweets
- ✔ People mentioning your project or web page in their comments on various websites and news stories online

It's important to remember that these backers, whether or not they ended up funding your project, are interested in your passion. Although there are many different types of social media and ways to stay in touch with backers, remember to pick the methods you're most comfortable with. If you don't like the brief nature of Twitter posts, don't use it as a tool for communicating with your community; stick to methods you like — perhaps e-mail messages or posts on your own blog.

After your campaign is over, I recommend committing to at least 30 minutes a week online updating your backers, whether or not your Kickstarter campaign was successful. That might mean posting a project update on your website or uploading new video snippets to your YouTube channel; it could be something as simple as re-tweeting something you think your backers would be interested in. Continue this update process throughout and beyond your project's lifespan.

Many Kickstarters continue to use their community developed through this process. Writer Dimitri Samarov completed a successful Kickstarter campaign in June 2012 for his book, *Hack: More Stories from a Chicago Cab,* a compilation of stories and sketches based on his work as a Chicago taxi driver. He previously released a successful first compilation, and this was his next series of stories.

Samarov raised over $6,600 through the campaign to fund production of this second book, expected for delivery in 2013. After the completion of his successful campaign, he has stayed in touch with his Kickstarter backers through e-mails gathered in the process to let those people interested in his work know about not only his Kickstarter campaign book, but also gallery shows for his original sketches and an audio CD of an assortment of tales. Each of these products has benefited from the continued momentum of keeping up with Kickstarter backers.

Fostering your community offline

Even though Kickstarter is a web-based crowdfunding site — and most of the communication tools I discuss in other chapters about soliciting backers are electronic — it doesn't mean this is the only way to build a community for your project.

Kickstarter is simply a way to begin — to give your concept or idea a quick start — a kick-start. After you've completed your campaign and communicated with backers about how to keep updated on your project, it's important to retain a human element to your outreach.

Below is a list of ideas for potential ways to build your community offline:

✔ **Invite all your backers in your town to join you at your favorite local pub or restaurant for a happy hour.** This is not to imply that you're hosting everyone or paying for everyone, just creating an opportunity for backers to come together at the same time and get to meet up.

✔ **Attend or organize gatherings around a topic or interest related to your project.** Speaking of meeting up, a great tool is www.meetup.com. This social networking site helps people interested in the same topic to find each other and meet up in real life at events and programs. If there is a Meetup group that matches the interests of your project, try attending it — and inviting other backers to come with you.

Figure 8-1 shows an example of a Meetup relevant to people interested in art, specifically painting and figure drawing.

✔ **Attend events by others in similar categories to your Kickstarter project.** In your community, look at the Calendar section of the local newspaper, search online for sites like www.patch.com, or pick up your free weekly entertainment guide if the city has one. Browse listings for events and stop by one or two, inviting a few backers to join you — and be sure to bring along information on your own project to share!

Figure 8-1: Use online tools like Meetup to build your community offline.

Delivering Rewards to Your Backers

When you come to the end of your campaign, if it's successful, you need to do a few tasks right away to ensure successful delivery of your backer rewards: Generate your Backer Report and survey your backers.

Downloading your Backer Report

To generate a report of all your backers and relevant data about their rewards, follow these steps:

1. **Go to your Dashboard on the main Kickstarter page.**

   You will see an overview of all Project Activity listed in several graphical forms. Figure 8-2 shows a sample Project Activity page.

2. **Print this entire page for your records.**

3. **On the top navigation bar, click Backer Report to see an aggregate of all your pledges, grouped by pledge amount; print this entire page as well for your records.**

   Figure 8-3 shows an example of an aggregated Backer Report. For each pledge level, you see a blue arrow and View Report link on the right.

Figure 8-2: This is how a Project Activity page looks at the conclusion of a project.

4. **Click View Report for your first backer level, as shown in Figure 8-4.**

   You see a list of all backers at that level and several key tools you will want to use: Generate Report, Message All, and Create a Survey. Figure 8-5 shows the various tools available inside your report.

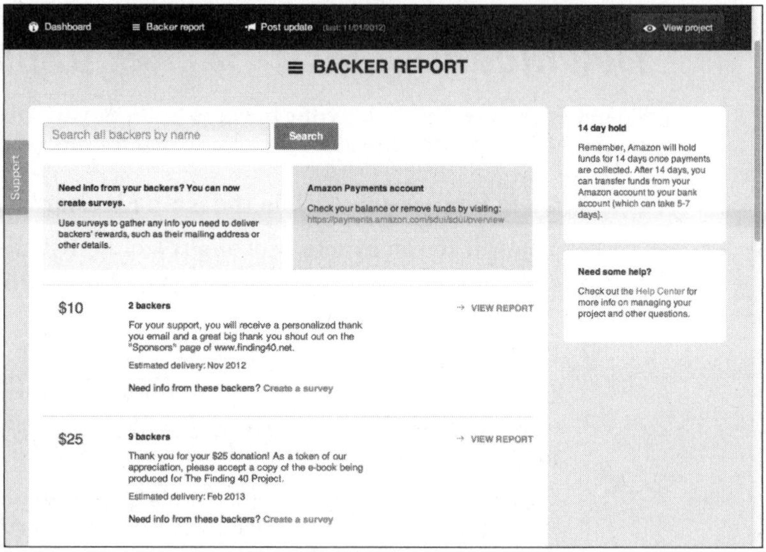

Figure 8-3: An aggregated Backer Report.

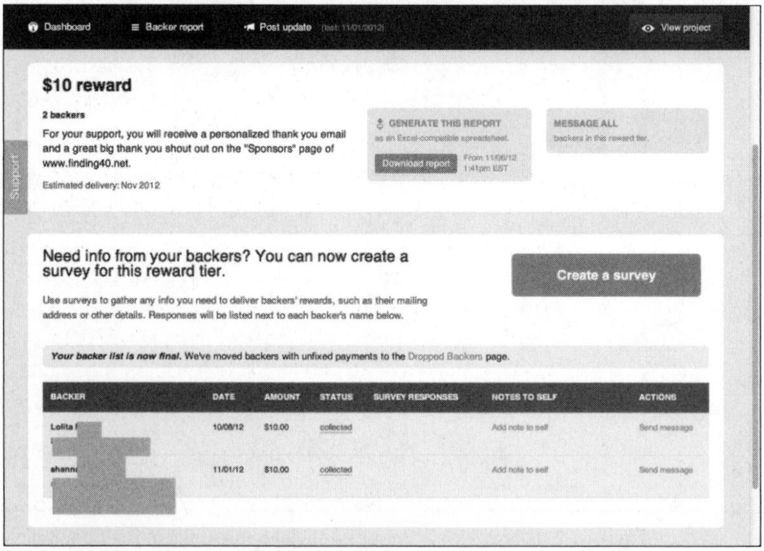

Figure 8-4: Drilling down to the first backer level.

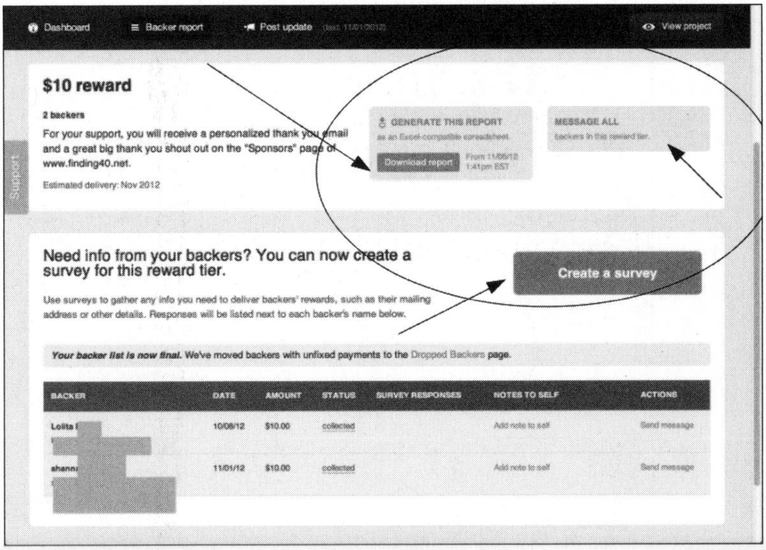

Figure 8-5: Tools available inside the Backer Report.

5. **Click the Download Report button near the top and center of the screen.**

   A pop-up window asks you to verify that you wish to download the report.

6. **Click Download again.**

   The information on backers in that level will download to your computer as a CSV (comma-separated values) format file, compatible with Microsoft Excel, Open Office Calc, and other spreadsheet programs. By default, the file is saved in your Downloads or My Downloads folder, depending on your computer.

7. **Click the Back button on your browser and repeat this same process for each of your individual backer levels.**

   Each file will download separately, organized by backer level. Figure 8-6 shows a sample Backer Report. Note that I deleted confidential backer information to show you the report in this book; the actual report you get is complete with full names and e-mail addresses.

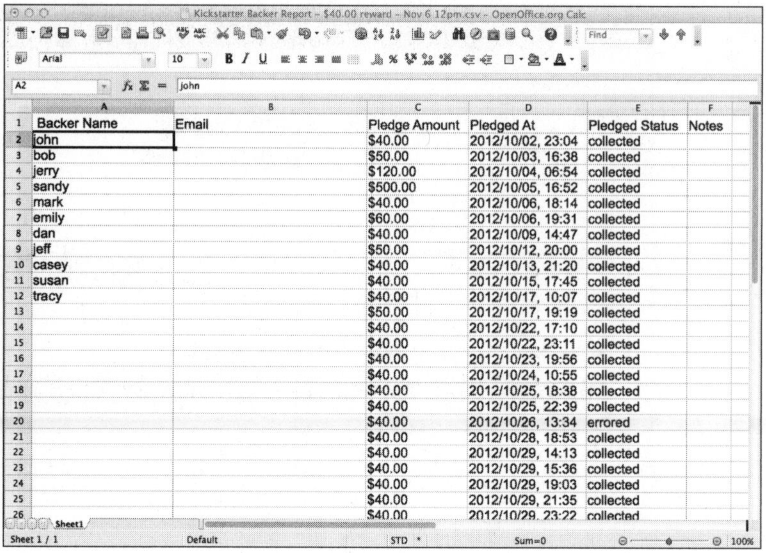

	Backer Name	Email	Pledge Amount	Pledged At	Pledged Status	Notes
2	john		$40.00	2012/10/02, 23:04	collected	
3	bob		$50.00	2012/10/03, 16:38	collected	
4	jerry		$120.00	2012/10/04, 06:54	collected	
5	sandy		$500.00	2012/10/05, 16:52	collected	
6	mark		$40.00	2012/10/06, 18:14	collected	
7	emily		$60.00	2012/10/06, 19:31	collected	
8	dan		$40.00	2012/10/09, 14:47	collected	
9	jeff		$50.00	2012/10/12, 20:00	collected	
10	casey		$40.00	2012/10/13, 21:20	collected	
11	susan		$40.00	2012/10/15, 17:45	collected	
12	tracy		$40.00	2012/10/17, 10:07	collected	
13			$50.00	2012/10/17, 19:19	collected	
14			$40.00	2012/10/22, 17:10	collected	
15			$40.00	2012/10/22, 23:11	collected	
16			$40.00	2012/10/23, 19:56	collected	
17			$40.00	2012/10/24, 10:55	collected	
18			$40.00	2012/10/25, 18:38	collected	
19			$40.00	2012/10/25, 22:39	collected	
20			$40.00	2012/10/26, 13:34	errored	
21			$40.00	2012/10/28, 18:53	collected	
22			$40.00	2012/10/29, 14:13	collected	
23			$40.00	2012/10/29, 15:36	collected	
24			$40.00	2012/10/29, 19:03	collected	
25			$40.00	2012/10/29, 21:35	collected	
26			$40.00	2012/10/29, 23:22	collected	

Figure 8-6: Sample Backer Report in CSV format.

Surveying your backers

After downloading all your Backer Reports and printing out your Project Activity pages, it's important to determine whether you have all the information you need from backers to deliver their rewards.

If everything you're offering can be delivered electronically (for example via e-mail), then the e-mail address each backer provided during their registration should be sufficient. However, if you're offering anything else (copies of products, special services, invitations to events, and so on), it's important to get the information required from backers as soon as possible.

To do that, you use Kickstarter's survey feature. This is not an opinion survey, but a survey to specifically gather required data from your backers. Figure 8-7 shows the Create a Survey button inside your Backer Report.

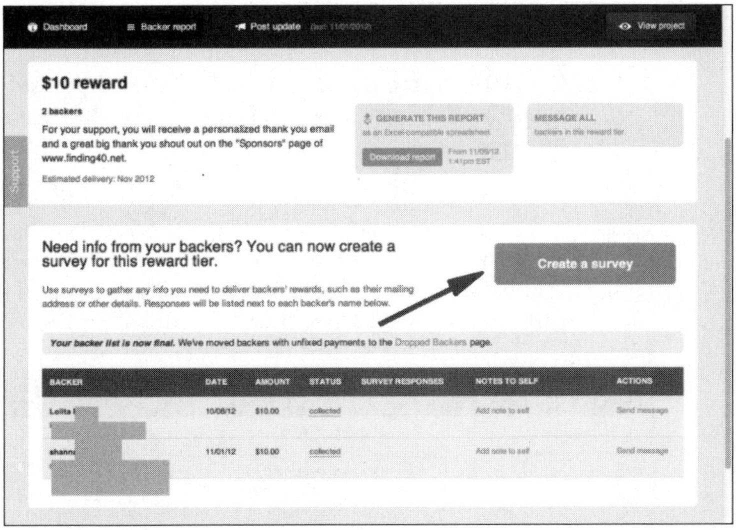

Figure 8-7: Create a Survey button.

The following steps walk you through the process of creating a survey:

1. **Click the Create a Survey button inside each individual level of Backer Report.**

   You see several boxes that enable you to request information from backers, as shown in Figure 8-8.

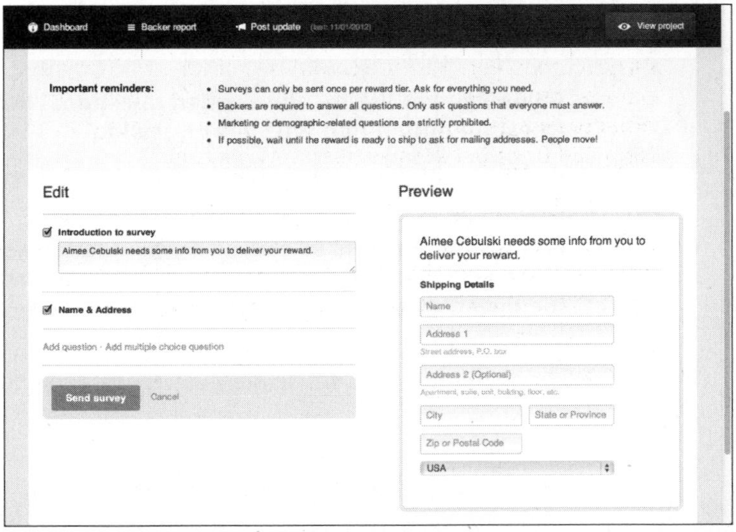

Figure 8-8: Creating a survey with the Backer Report tools.

2. **Select the Introduction to Survey option and type a short explanation of why you're conducting the survey.**

3. **Keep the Name & Address box selected (it's selected by default) if you need to request a backer's mailing address.**

   Ask for addresses if you're sending backers a product.

   If there are special requests or other needs — for example, sizes of T-shirts or favorite varieties of a food product you're producing, there is also an option to add as many other questions as you'd like (as shown in Figure 8-9).

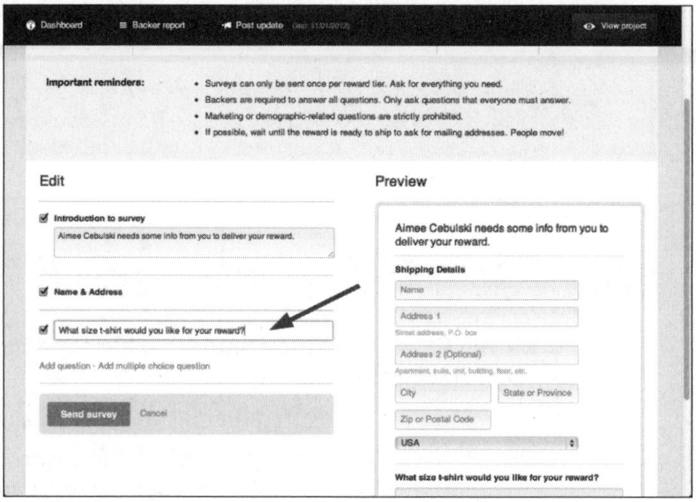

Figure 8-9: Adding a custom question into a backer survey.

4. **If you need to ask an open-ended question, click the Add Question option and type your question.**

   In the resulting survey, backers can enter their response in a text box.

5. **If you want backers to choose from a limited set of answers, click Add Multiple Choice Question and fill out the question and options on the screen that appears.**

   This is a good option to use if, for example, your T-shirt sizes are limited to small, medium, large, and extra large.

You don't want backers to respond with sizes you don't have, like extra small or extra-extra large).

6. **Review your survey information to make sure it's complete and accurate, and then click Send Survey.**

As your backers respond to your survey questions, their information will be updated in the Backer Report. To check how many backers have replied, click Backer Report from your main Dashboard (again, in the top center black bar). There, you will be able to determine how many people have replied to your survey and who has not yet responded. Once you get all the information needed from all the backers in one level, re-download the backer report (as outlined earlier in this chapter) and replace your older version with this newer one which has more information.

You may need to complete this process several times or send reminder e-mails to your backers to get the information needed. Don't give up! Be sure to re-send survey requests until all your backers have sent the information you've requested.

Keeping Up with Kickstarter

Once you've completed your project, surveyed all your backers, downloaded complete Backer Reports, and posted your final update, you're done with the Kickstarter page, right? Wrong!

To stay connected with Kickstarter and all the great projects (including some that might be a good fit with yours), you can regularly visit the Kickstarter Blog (www.kickstarter.com/blog). It's a good idea to visit the blog at least once a week for the posts related to This Week in Kickstarter, highlighting cool new concepts, projects, and milestones. Figure 8-10 shows a sample blog entry.

Beyond getting the weekly update, browse around for featured projects and other news from the Kickstarter staff. If you see a project that you like or could be affiliated with yours, be sure to click and back it. Also, each blog entry is associated with a Kickstarter author. When you click an entry that you're interested in, click the author's name (highlighted in blue), to see what other projects he or she is interested in or has backed (as seen in Figure 8-11).

Whether or not your particular campaign was successful, keeping up with Kickstarter this way can give you inspiration for your next project.

Figure 8-10: Sample Kickstarter blog entry.

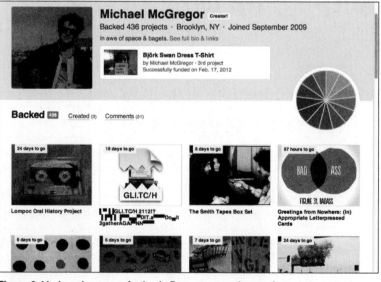

Figure 8-11: Jumping to an Author's Page to see other projects.

Chapter 9

Ten Unique Reward Ideas

In This Chapter

▶ Comparing ten real-world rewards for backers

▶ Discovering what makes a reward unique

*T*his chapter examines some creative ideas for one of the most important parts of your Kickstarter campaign: backer rewards. People will likely want something in return for their pledges, and in this chapter, you find ten intriguing ideas from a variety of Kickstarter campaigns — both successful and unsuccessful. Even if the campaign may not have reached its ultimate funding goal (for whatever reason), the campaign creator may have come up with some clever rewards for backers, and they are included here for that reason.

"Cover Me!": Featuring Backers on Your Cover

If you're creating something with a cover — like a book, comic, album, or magazine — what about incorporating your backers' names or photos into the cover art?

If there is an opportunity to work a backer's image into the art, that could be a lot of fun! Perhaps you could feature his or her photograph on the back cover as an original backer?

Remember that your cover is one important way to sell your finished product, so you can't let a backer's image interfere with the message of the product; you'll need to work with your designer to integrate the backer's photo cleverly into the art. Perhaps a fun "Where's Waldo?" type of look? Or maybe you work the backer's name into the image with a fun typeface or font.

This type of backer reward should be limited in quantity, unless you're making your entire front or back cover about your backers. I would recommend limiting this reward to maybe 2–5 backers total.

Figure 9-1 shows an example of a campaign organized by VOTA, a band that used Kickstarter to raise funds for recording an album. For backers who donated $45 or more, VOTA offered to feature their photos in a mosaic on the album cover. By choosing a mosaic, VOTA could offer this reward to up to 675 backers. (It's worth noting that, if 675 people had chosen this reward, the band would have basically doubled its fundraising goal. See Chapter 3 for details about balancing your fundraising goal with your rewards.) VOTA was also smart to consider how backers' photos would be featured in the cover design in the reward description. This way, backers could have clear expectations for how their photos would appear — and VOTA could plan the album cover ahead of time.

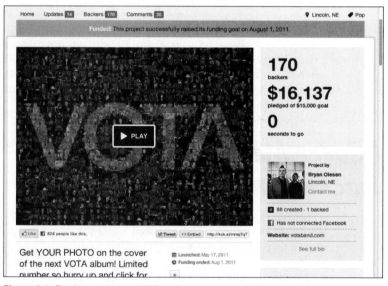

Figure 9-1: Backer option on VOTA album cover at $45 backer level.

"The Shirt Off Your Back": Offering T-Shirts

T-shirts have always been a popular giveaway item. Whether you're running in a race, participating in a charity walk, or supporting a school function, a commemorative T-shirt is often a desirable reward for a pledge.

You should consider a T-shirt as a backer reward for several reasons:

- ✔ T-shirts are often inexpensive to produce.

- ✔ You can produce a large or small quantity.

- ✔ T-shirts promote your brand/product identity outside of Kickstarter.

- ✔ T-shirts are gender- and age-neutral.

Be sure to enter your T-shirt production costs into your overall Kickstarter budget if you're going to use this as a reward. (See Chapter 3 for budgeting.) The only exception is if a kind friend or business associate is donating the shirts *and* their production. (But don't forget the shipping.)

Because the T-shirt is also a familiar way to promote your brand or product well beyond Kickstarter, be sure to come up with a design that will communicate your message to someone who may know nothing about it.

Figure 9-2 shows a sample reward T-shirt.

In this instance, backers get T-shirts as a thank-you for their support to make the podcasts happen. As a bonus, the T-shirts themselves feature a cool design and might be something the potential backer would want to order anyway, even if it didn't help support a creative project.

Figure 9-2: Pollyanna Cowgirl Records Podcast offered a T-shirt reward at the $15 backer level.

"Naming Rights": Including a Backer as a Character

Have you ever wanted to be a character in a movie, book, or TV show? It's likely your backers have wanted that too — at least to have a character named after them! This reward is a creative way to have your backer be forever linked to your project.

If your project is a work of fiction, how about naming a character after a backer? This is usually reserved for a higher-end backer, unless you have hundreds of characters to choose from.

Figure 9-3 shows a high-end reward for the Plunder game, where a backer gets to "become" a character. Here are a few notable points about this example:

- ✔ The reward description spells out details about how the character would be included in the game.

- ✔ The creator mentions up-front the right to reject backer ideas for the character.

The Grand Treasure, however, is the most special of them all. Most grant incredible abilities to their holders, and they're all very valuable. However, there's a catch: there's only one available on the board at a time, and it's surrounded by **Curse Spaces**. To get to it, a character has to hit a **Curse Space** on the way in, and one on the way out. It's risky, but the payoff is enormous. Once it's nabbed, other players have to wait several turns for a new **Grand Treasure** to spawn.

Estimated delivery: Jun 2013
Add $10 to ship outside the US

Pledge $10,000 or more

⭕ 0 backers   Limited (1 of 1 left)

PIRATE KING/QUEEN TIER: For this unbelievable pledge, you will get the royal treatment. We will fly you down to meet us for a meet and greet, a fancy dinner with the people who helped work on the game, and a special session of Plunder! with David Burner, the creator of the game. You will become a character in every copy of the game, and the creator will personally design a full custom team of six player cards for you, as well as a full custom board especially for you! You will receive large-scale, framed, signed prints of all your artwork! You will also receive a special thank you message printed in the manual of the game! You will also get the sticker pack, the mini-print, the t-shirt, the hoodie and 10 copies of the game! *The creator reserves the right to refuse ideas that involve graphic violence, nudity, and other explicit themes.

Estimated delivery: Jun 2013

Figure 9-3: Character naming reward at $10,000 level in Plunder.

"Autograph, Please": Signing Your Work

An original author's/artist's signature on any work will make it more valuable than an unsigned piece. Whether or not your book goes on to become a bestseller or your gallery show leads to worldwide acclaim, giving your backers a signed copy of your finished piece enhances value without costing you anything.

When considering your backer levels, look at the idea of creating two offers, one slightly higher than the other, that are differentiated by a signature. Even if one offer is only $5 more than the other, if a larger percentage of backers go for the signed copy, you'll reach your Kickstarter goal faster.

Figure 9-4 below shows rewards for a signed copy of an album, plus a slightly higher reward for people who want the album before it becomes available on iTunes.

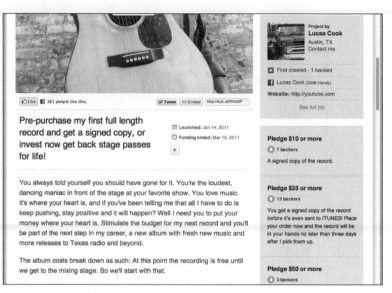

Figure 9-4: Signed copies of an album by Lucas Cook.

"Casting Call": Rewarding Backers with Bit Parts

Do you think some of your backers dream of seeing themselves on the big or small screen? Do you have aspiring actors in your network of friends? The idea of casting someone in your project is a fun and engaging reward idea.

Depending on the backer level, you can offer a number of walk-on roles for your project. Perhaps you can include these backers as extras or crowd fillers, or a backer could walk through a scene to create action. Whatever the role, giving your backers a chance to actually be *in* your project definitely connects them to it for the long haul — and will encourage them to share the project with others.

Figure 9-5 shows a backer offer for a role as an extra on the *Oblivion* web series.

Be an extra in a show

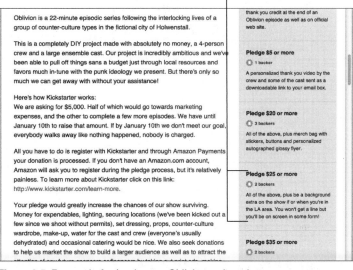

Oblivion is a 22-minute episodic series following the interlocking lives of a group of counter-culture types in the fictional city of Holwenstall.

This is a completely DIY project made with absolutely no money, a 4-person crew and a large ensemble cast. Our project is incredibly ambitious and we've been able to pull off things sans a budget just through local resources and favors much in-tune with the punk ideology we present. But there's only so much we can get away with without your assistance!

Here's how Kickstarter works:
We are asking for $5,000. Half of which would go towards marketing expenses, and the other to complete a few more episodes. We have until January 10th to raise that amount. If by January 10th we don't meet our goal, everybody walks away like nothing happened, nobody is charged.

All you have to do is register with Kickstarter and through Amazon Payments your donation is processed. If you don't have an Amazon.com account, Amazon will ask you to register during the pledge process, but it's relatively painless. To learn more about Kickstarter click on this link:
http://www.kickstarter.com/learn-more.

Your pledge would greatly increase the chances of our show surviving. Money for expendables, lighting, securing locations (we've been kicked out a few since we shoot without permits), set dressing, props, counter-culture wardrobe, make-up, water for the cast and crew (everyone's usually dehydrated) and occasional catering would be nice. We also seek donations to help us market the show to build a larger audience as well as to attract the

thank you credit at the end of an Oblivion episode as well as on official web site.

Pledge $5 or more
1 backer
A personalized thank you video by the crew and some of the cast sent as a downloadable link to your email box.

Pledge $20 or more
3 backers
All of the above, plus merch bag with stickers, buttons and personalized autographed glossy flyer.

Pledge $25 or more
2 backers
All of the above, plus be a background extra on the show if or when you're in the LA area. You won't get a line but you'll be on screen in some form!

Pledge $35 or more
2 backers

Figure 9-5: Extra role for backer on *Oblivion* web series.

"Curtain Call": Sharing Tickets to Your Show

Many Kickstarter campaigns have to do with production of a show or performance — live theater, performance art, concerts, and so on. If you're using Kickstarter to produce a live event, how about offering free seats to your backers?

In reality, it's not a free seat, because backers are pledging an amount to support your campaign as a whole. However, if you word your reward with "Free Tickets," "Complimentary Entry," and so forth, backers feel like they are getting something for free — and they are: They don't have to shell out for a ticket at the event.

When creating a backer reward that includes free seats or tickets for an event, be sure your reward level at least covers what you would hope to sell those seats for. For example, if tickets to your concert will cost $20 each and you have a backer reward that includes two tickets to the show, make sure that backer reward is priced at $40 or more.

Figure 9-6 shows tickets included to a production of *Screwtape*. In this campaign, backers who give more to the production get extra perks with their tickets, such as a choice of which performance to attend.

Matinee tickets reward

Ticekts for the performance time of your choice

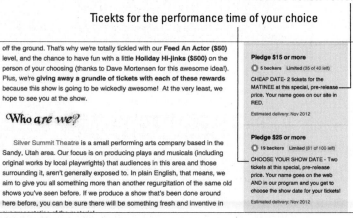

off the ground. That's why we're totally tickled with our **Feed An Actor ($50)** level, and the chance to have fun with a little **Holiday Hi-jinks ($500)** on the person of your choosing (thanks to Dave Mortensen for this awesome idea!). Plus, we're **giving away a grundle of tickets with each of these rewards** because this show is going to be wickedly awesome! At the very least, we hope to see you at the show.

Who are we?

Silver Summit Theatre is a small performing arts company based in the Sandy, Utah area. Our focus is on producing plays and musicals (including original works by local playwrights) that audiences in this area and those surrounding it, aren't generally exposed to. In plain English, that means, we aim to give you all something more than another regurgitation of the same old shows you've seen before. If we produce a show that's been done around here before, you can be sure there will be something fresh and inventive in

Pledge $15 or more

5 backers   Limited (35 of 40 left)

CHEAP DATE- 2 tickets for the MATINEE at this special, pre-release price. Your name goes on our site in RED.

Estimated delivery: Nov 2012

Pledge $25 or more

19 backers   Limited (81 of 100 left)

CHOOSE YOUR SHOW DATE - Two tickets at this special, pre-release price. Your name goes on the web AND in our program and you get to choose the show date for your tickets!

Estimated delivery: Nov 2012

Figure 9-6: Backer rewards including tickets to production of *Screwtape*.

"Hero Worship": Making a Backer the Hero of Your Project

This is a bit of a twist on an earlier idea, naming rights, but it applies most specifically to books or comics with a true hero or champion.

If you have one level of backer rewards for character naming, perhaps you have a second tier, with even more limited availability, where your backer could be the hero of the story.

For those producing a comic, this a true opportunity for one of your backers to become a superhero. You can work with your backer(s) to determine what special powers he or she would have, how the character would look, and even brainstorm the outcome of the character's adventure!

Because this type of commitment involves a lot of interaction with the backer, make sure the requirements are outlined clearly in your rewards and limit the number of rewards available at this level. The Hyper-Heroes project, shown in Figure 9-7, limited its hero reward to three backers and set the backer level at $5,000.

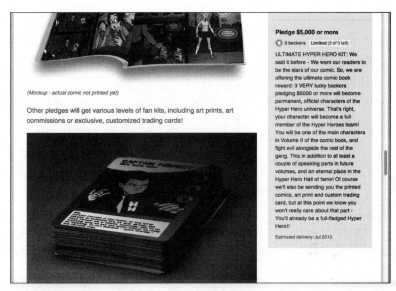

(Mockup - actual comic not printed yet)

Other pledges will get various levels of fan kits, including art prints, art commissions or exclusive, customized trading cards!

Pledge $5,000 or more

0 backers   Limited (3 of 3 left)

ULTIMATE HYPER HERO KIT: We said it before - We want our readers to be the stars of our comic. So, we are offering the ultimate comic book reward: 3 VERY lucky backers pledging $5000 or more will become permanent, official characters of the Hyper Hero universe. That's right, your character will become a full member of the Hyper Heroes team! You will be one of the main characters in Volume II of the comic book, and fight evil alongside the rest of the gang. This is in addition to at least a couple of speaking parts in future volumes, and an eternal place in the Hyper Hero Hall of fame! Of course we'll also be sending you the printed comics, art print and custom trading card, but at this point we know you won't really care about that part - You'll already be a full-fledged Hyper Hero!!

Estimated delivery: Jul 2013

Figure 9-7: The Hyper-Heroes reward: A backer becomes a hero character at $5,000 level.

"Dinner Guest": Meeting Your Backers in Person

Food is always a great way to connect with others. Try using it as a creative backer reward! Most likely, many of your backers will be within your home city or close by.

There are two ideas here for using food as a reward for backers:

- ✔ Offering to cook a meal for a select backer at his or her home, or host a group of backers at your home
- ✔ Hosting a meal/reception/happy hour for a large group of backers all at once

Each type of food-related reward has its own benefits. If you host a small, intimate dinner party, you have the option of really showing your backers how much you appreciate their support with a home-cooked meal. Of course, you need to have space to host a dinner party and the skills needed to pull this off!

If a home-cooked, small dinner party is not an option, another approach is to host a dinner at a local restaurant or cater a get-together at an appropriate location. You can open up this level of reward to more backers (keep in mind that it will probably be more expensive than offering a home-cooked meal).

It's important to consider the costs of each option — and be sure to add those costs to your overall project budget if you're going to offer these rewards.

Again, be sure to limit the number of backers at these levels and ensure that you can deliver on the end result! You must also clearly lay out the size of group for each reward — and specify the distance you're willing to travel for fulfillment.

Figure 9-8 shows a $250 backer reward from my campaign, The Finding 40 Project, offering a home-cooked meal.

Figure 9-8: Home-cooked meal at $250 reward level for The Finding 40 Project.

"Sign Me Up": Offering Subscriptions

If your Kickstarter campaign is launching a series that might continue month after month or year after year, consider offering an ongoing subscription or membership to backers.

This type of reward encourages backers to believe in the project long term and also allows you to basically pre-sell subscriptions, ensuring readership or membership beyond your launch period.

Again, as with the tickets idea, be sure that the contribution at this backer level truly covers the cost of an ongoing subscription — and that you spell out the length of the subscription (usually a year but some subscriptions run for two years). Other subscription-style rewards offer a set number of issues instead of a timeframe-based subscription.

As an example, if you're creating a quarterly magazine with an annual subscription rate of $40, I would recommend that any reward offering a subscription start no lower than $40, ideally closer to $100.

Figure 9-9 shows *Thirty-Two* magazine and a backer level that features a year-long subscription to the publication.

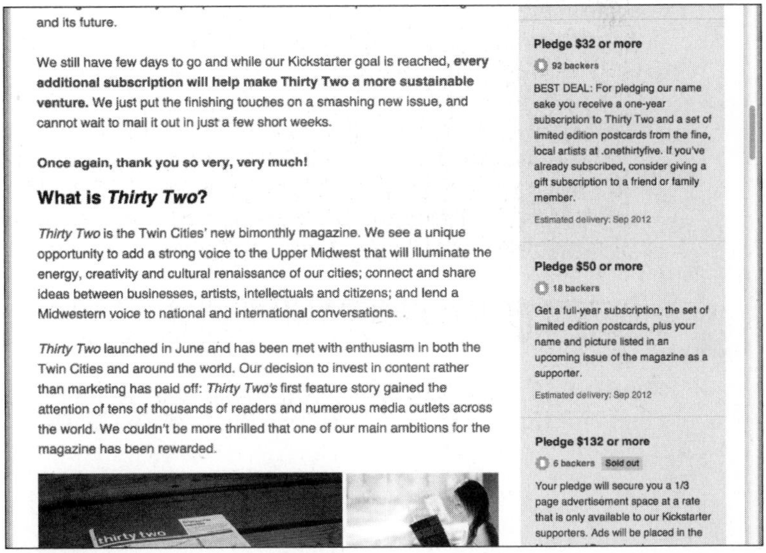

and its future.

We still have few days to go and while our Kickstarter goal is reached, **every additional subscription will help make Thirty Two a more sustainable venture.** We just put the finishing touches on a smashing new issue, and cannot wait to mail it out in just a few short weeks.

Once again, thank you so very, very much!

What is *Thirty Two*?

Thirty Two is the Twin Cities' new bimonthly magazine. We see a unique opportunity to add a strong voice to the Upper Midwest that will illuminate the energy, creativity and cultural renaissance of our cities; connect and share ideas between businesses, artists, intellectuals and citizens; and lend a Midwestern voice to national and international conversations.

Thirty Two launched in June and has been met with enthusiasm in both the Twin Cities and around the world. Our decision to invest in content rather than marketing has paid off: *Thirty Two's* first feature story gained the attention of tens of thousands of readers and numerous media outlets across the world. We couldn't be more thrilled that one of our main ambitions for the magazine has been rewarded.

Pledge $32 or more

92 backers

BEST DEAL: For pledging our name sake you receive a one-year subscription to Thirty Two and a set of limited edition postcards from the fine, local artists at .onethirtyfive. If you've already subscribed, consider giving a gift subscription to a friend or family member.

Estimated delivery: Sep 2012

Pledge $50 or more

18 backers

Get a full-year subscription, the set of limited edition postcards, plus your name and picture listed in an upcoming issue of the magazine as a supporter.

Estimated delivery: Sep 2012

Pledge $132 or more

6 backers   Sold out

Your pledge will secure you a 1/3 page advertisement space at a rate that is only available to our Kickstarter supporters. Ads will be placed in the

Figure 9-9: $32 backer level at *Thirty-Two* magazine, featuring a year-long subscription.

"Fly Me to the Moon": Bringing an Out-of-Town Backer to an Event

Well, maybe not to the moon . . . but how about to your premiere, or to your project's launch party?

Bringing a backer in from out of town to support your project definitely adds a sense of drama or excitement to the launch. If you have a backer who has wanted to see you anyway and lives out of town, this is a great way to combine a visit with a pledge to back your project.

Another option is to create a vacation package around your premiere or launch. Talk to managers at local hotels and see if they might be interested in donating a room night or two to your project in exchange for publicity or exposure on your website or at your event.

Do you have unused reward miles or credit-card reward points? Consider offering them up as part of a reward package as well; you could create a getaway package to visit your town. See if you can get donated or discounted tickets to local attractions to round out the package. This might be appealing to a backer you don't even know but who is interested in visiting your city!

Again, remember that anything you have to purchase for this reward level needs to be entered into your budget against your project's bottom line. This type of reward needs to be priced correctly as well.

If you need to spend $400 on an average plane ticket plus $500 on hotel rooms and event attraction tickets for a package reward, don't price your reward level any lower than $1,000. Ideally, you want this package to help generate revenue for your project, not just cover hard costs.

The more resources you can get discounted or donated for this type of reward, the greater the revenue you can generate.

Figure 9-10 shows a backer reward that features hotel accommodations for the Dig South Interactive Conference and Expo.

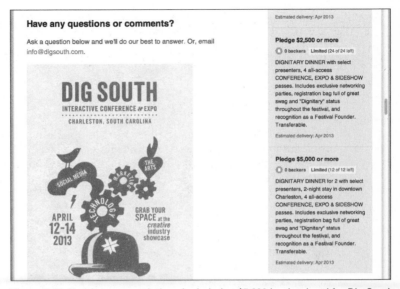

Figure 9-10: Hotel accommodations included at $5,000 backer level for Dig South Interactive Conference and Expo.

Chapter 10

Ten Resources to Help with Your Campaign

· ·

In This Chapter

▶ Learning from Kickstarter itself and other Kickstarter projects

▶ Putting together a budget and a business plan

▶ Writing clear campaign copy

▶ Designing a website for your campaign

▶ Taking great photos

▶ Promoting your project and or a supporting event

· ·

So far, hopefully, this book has given you lots of ideas and tips for making your Kickstarter campaign a success. There are countless other places you can go for inspiration and guidance. In this chapter, I outline ten additional ways you can boost your campaign by seeking outside information and developing potential skills you need for your Kickstarter campaign.

Finding Kickstarter-Specific Resources

Thanks to Kickstarter's explosive success, there are now a number of websites specifically developed to help you manage your campaign and reward deliveries. Here are a few of my favorites:

> ✔ **Kicktraq** (www.kicktraq.com): Allows you to monitor your campaign's status and forecasts campaign outcomes. Kicktraq also offers other campaign tips and a regularly

updated blog. Figure 10-1 shows a sample tracking and forecast for a Kickstarter campaign in progress, "Take the Plunge."

✔ **BackerKit** (www.backerkit.com)**:** This new website gives Kickstarter campaign owners the basic tools and tips to deliver rewards to backers. For many Kickstarter campaign owners, failure to deliver rewards has been a big issue. BackerKit is an option if you find yourself overwhelmed with delivery. Figure 10-2 shows the BackerKit site, where you can start learning more about this service.

BackerKit costs money. If you plan to use it for delivering your rewards, be sure to add the hard cost into your budget.

✔ **The Kickstarter Tumblr page** (http://kickstarter. tumblr.com)**:** An ongoing blog written by the team behind Kickstarter with interesting tidbits and notes about ongoing campaigns and successful project tips.

Figure 10-1: Kicktraq page showing progress and likelihood of the "Take the Plunge" project's success.

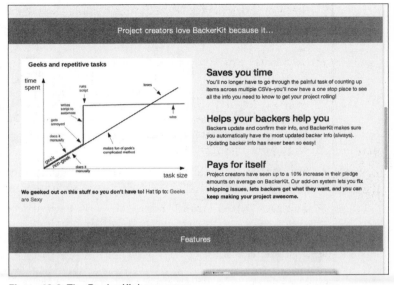

Figure 10-2: The BackerKit home page.

Learning from Other Kickstarter Stories

In Chapter 2, I discuss reviewing other Kickstarter's campaigns as a way to gauge your own potential campaign and get a sense for what others in your potential category are doing. There are a number of great web and news sites where you can also search for keywords like "Kickstarter" and see what others have written about Kickstarter campaigns:

> ✔ **Mashable** (www.mashable.com): This site frequently has stories about ongoing campaigns and ideas from other users, as well as reporter commentary. Check back often and search "Kickstarter" on the main page for most recent stories, as shown in Figure 10-3.

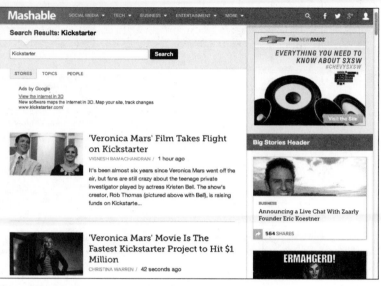

Figure 10-3: Mashable home page with "Kickstarter" search.

✔ **The Huffington Post** (www.huffingtonpost.com): This site often aggregates news from a variety of sources all over the web. As with Mashable.com, simply enter **Kickstarter** in the search box at the top of the page to see what stories are trending that relate to Kickstarter projects around the country.

Budgeting for Your Project

Chapter 3 reviews the steps in creating a successful Kickstarter campaign budget. In the chapter I recommend using a spreadsheet-type program such as Microsoft Excel. If you are not familiar with how to use spreadsheets, check out the tips for several versions of Excel at Dummies.com. Simply type the version you have (such as Excel 2013) into the search box. Or check out *Excel For Dummies* by Greg Harvey.

If you don't have access to Microsoft Excel and don't want to purchase a copy of the software, there are other, free resources such as the OpenOffice Calc program, that offer the basic spreadsheet functions you'll need, such as tabulating data and performing basic calculations.

Figure 10-4 shows the `OpenOffice.org` web page for its Calc program. OpenOffice is actually an entire suite of products that also includes a word processor and a slideshow program.

Figure 10-4: Calc is a good alternative to Excel if you need a spreadsheet program.

Making a Business Plan

Remember, Kickstarter is all about getting a project up and running — giving it that proverbial "kick-start." Just having a successful Kickstarter campaign doesn't mean your project will actually *be* successful. It's up to you to make good use of the support and money from your backers to make your project into a viable venture.

Because each individual campaign and product is inherently different, there is no one-size-fits-all model business plan to follow, but you should create at least a basic business plan that lays out how you will maintain and make money with your project.

Start your web search for business plan resources here:

✔ **Dummies.com** (www.dummies.com): From the home page, do a search for *business plan* to find articles that can help you determine what to include in your business plan and how to monitor your progress based on your plan. For a more comprehensive guide on how to create and manage a winning business plan, check out *Business Plans For Dummies,* 3rd Edition, by Paul Tiffany, Steven D. Peterson, and Colin Barrow.

✔ **Small Business Administration** (www.sba.gov): The SBA is dedicated to helping small businesses succeed, and your Kickstarter campaign is its own small business. This comprehensive website even has a step-by-step free tool for making your own business plan, as shown in Figure 10-5. You can access this free tool by clicking the Starting and Managing tab on the SBA home page and then clicking the Create Your Business Plan heading on the next page.

✔ **Bplans** (www.bplans.com): This website is designed for a variety of types of businesses, with lots of options when it comes to creating your own business plan. You can also find links here to tools such as LivePlan, which is business plan development software for purchase (as a monthly subscription ranging from $11 – $20), as shown in Figure 10-6.

Figure 10-5: The Build Your Business Plan tool on sba.gov.

Figure 10-6: LivePlan software available for purchase.

Writing Well

Throughout this book I call attention to the need to tell your Kickstarter story through words and video. If you are not a professional writer — or need some help with basic copy editing — there are several outstanding resources out there.

A classic tool in almost every writer's toolkit is *The Elements of Style* by William Strunk Jr. and E. B. White. This pocket-sized but powerful guide explains basic grammar, principles for composing clear and effective prose, and how to avoid misusing or misspelling words and expressions that often trap the unwary. An afternoon spent reading this slim guide can help you improve your writing. *The Elements of Style* is a gem if you need help with turning your ideas into text or using terms properly. You can often find this book for sale new or used. Figure 10-7 shows used copies available for $3.68 on Amazon.com.

Another tool for writing assistance is an online platform like Wordy (`https://wordy.com/copy-editing/`), where you can upload your draft and receive feedback and edits from professional editors and copywriters. This can be helpful if you feel stuck in the writing process or are struggling to make transitions between ideas. Wordy is a paid service, so if you are going to use this to help write your Kickstarter descriptions or other materials, be sure to add the cost into your overall budget.

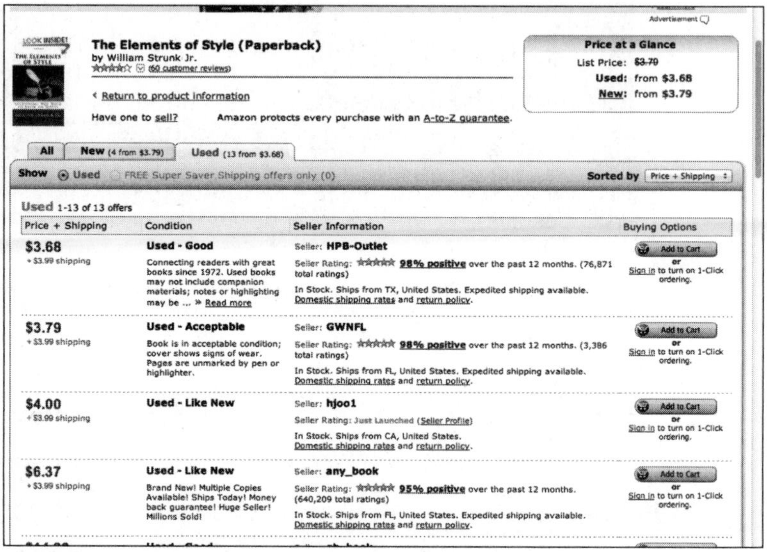

Figure 10-7: *The Elements of Style* available from only $3.68.

Copywriting Well

Copywriting is writing that's focused on advertising or publicity. You are copywriting for your campaign page when you write your short blurb or your long description (see Chapter 2) or write text for a website or blog that helps to support your campaign. (See the upcoming section in this chapter for help with a website.)

If you're daunted by the idea of writing promotional copy for a website — or if you've never done a single blog post — several good web-based tools can get you in the swing of it.

Copy Blogger (`www.copyblogger.com`) is a website created originally by blogger Brian Clark in 2006 to help others struggling with content creation.

The site prides itself on being able to teach anyone how to create "killer content." This could be extremely helpful to you if you are unsure about what to post in order to attract attention and drive traffic to your project's campaign page and website.

The Copy Blogger website offers some content for free. Although you have to pay to access its premium services, such as content marketing software and web hosting, these could be worthwhile expenses if you are acquiring skills that will help you grow your backer base. Remember to add any such paid services to your project's list of hard costs.

Figure 10-8 shows recent posts on the Copy Blogger site, where you are free to browse to get content and copy ideas from others around the web:

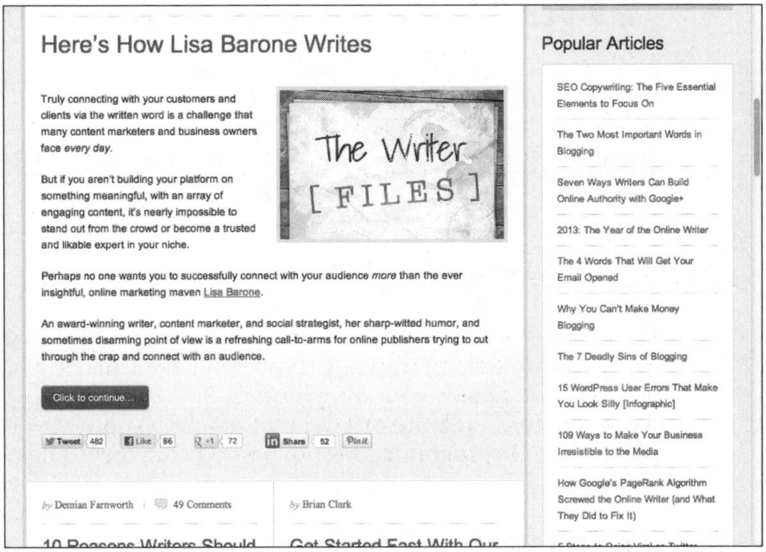

Figure 10-8: Content ideas on the Copy Blogger website.

Another tried-and-true tool for getting started on copywriting (or if you're already writing but stuck) is a good old-fashioned thesaurus. Of course, as a full-fledged member of the digital age, you might want to check out a few options that don't require you to crack open a giant volume:

✔ **Use the Thesaurus function on your word-processing software.** If you find yourself repeating the same word or struggling to communicate your idea, let technology help you! Type in the word you are trying to work around and see what other options pop up.

✔ **If you're a visual thinker, try using a website like the ThinkMap Visual Thesaurus** (www.visualthesaurus.com). This type of tool maps out word associations visually. You're directed to a series of possible connected words based on your original search term. You are able to drill not only down, but also around, in all directions, to find the right fit. Figure 10-9 shows the Visual Thesaurus website.

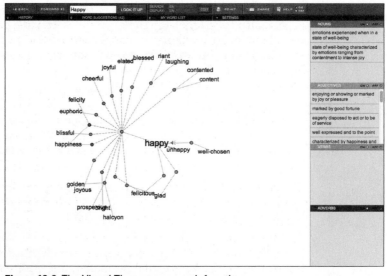

Figure 10-9: The Visual Thesaurus search function.

Writing Press Releases

In Chapters 6 and 8, I talk about getting the word out about your campaign, potentially reaching out to bloggers and writers that might cover your industry or neighborhood.

If you've never worked with a reporter before or sent out a press release, the prospect of tooting your own horn might seem a bit overwhelming. It's really not! Reporters are always looking for good stories and community activities, and if you have created a compelling call to action for your backers, that tells a good chunk of your Kickstarter story right there.

You may want to send press materials to reporters who would be able to write a story in time to benefit your campaign. See Chapter 6 for more details about paying to promote your Kickstarter campaign and making sure you advertise in a vehicle that fits your timeline.

A concise press release that announces your Kickstarter project, funding goal, end date, and relevant links to websites or other content can be a great way to communicate with bloggers and writers.

Three stellar resources are

- ✔ **Public Relations Society of America** (`www.prsa.org`): Learn about training programs and events that can help you build a press release. PRSA also has a student chapter called PRSSA, also found through the main PRSA website; you may be able to locate a chapter in your town and find a student willing to help you with PR for your campaign to boost his or her résumé.

- ✔ **PRWeb** (`www.prweb.com`): PRWeb is primarily an online tool for disseminating your press release to a large audience. Although this service might not be a good fit for your project, the site has excellent articles, such as "What is a Press Release?" and "How to Write a Successful Press Release," as shown in Figure 10-10.

  The site even has a free white paper available for download, called "An Expert Guide to Writing Great Online News Releases," that goes into even more depth.

- ✔ **AP Stylebook** (`http://apstylebook.com`): The Associated Press Stylebook is *the* Bible for anyone who writes for journalists or the media. A perennial bestseller, this book explains the guidelines for writing in news style, giving your press release a greater chance at getting picked up. The website gives you information on purchasing the most recent version as well as an interactive "Ask the Editor" section that lets you search thousands of queries to zero in on dilemmas of writing style, as shown in Figure 10-11.

Figure 10-10: Tips and techniques from PRWeb.

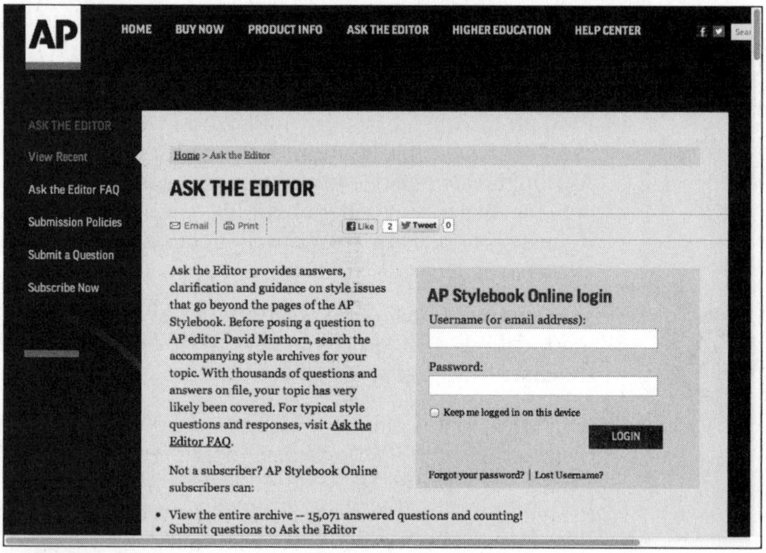

Figure 10-11: "Ask the Editor" feature on AP Stylebook.

Building a Basic Website

In addition to your Kickstarter campaign page, I recommend that you create at least a basic website for your Kickstarter project. Ideally, you have the website up and running before your campaign launches. Even if your site goes live after your campaign begins, you can still use it as a tool to communicate with backers when the campaign is over.

Your project website is a vital tool for connecting with a large number of people at once. Similar to your actual Kickstarter campaign, your project website needs to communicate the basics of your overall idea and passions. Each project is unique, but at the very minimum, you should think about building a site with the following categories of information:

✔ About the project

✔ Inspiration or background

✔ About you

✔ Photos or videos of the project

✔ Any links to the project in the news or blogs

Figure 10-12 shows the website for Creita, a company that creates innovative wire-mesh jewelry that can be molded into a variety of shapes. Creita had a successful Kickstarter campaign, raising funds to participate in fashion shows and events and getting the company on its way to a full production run. Notice how Creita has a website that mimics many of the things required in a good Kickstarter campaign, including strong visuals, videos, a backstory, and press mentions. Note that the site is not particularly complex — and now features a Shop button to allow direct user purchases.

Figure 10-13 is an excellent, straightforward website that mirrors a currently running Kickstarter campaign for "Powered by Green Smoothies." Filmmaker Sergei Boutenko is hoping to raise $50,000 for a full-length documentary showcasing the health effects of all-green smoothies on a variety of individuals, including athletes. The website hits on several of the key elements, including About, Events, Photos, and Videos. This site is primarily blog-driven, meaning that most of the content comes from the user posting updates and personal comments that highlight the filmmaker's passion.

Figure 10-12: Creita website with good examples of basic categories.

Figure 10-13: "Powered by Green Smoothies" filmmaker's website.

Of course, there are entire books, courses, and even college degrees on website design, but you don't need to be an expert on website design and maintenance. A basic site can be very helpful for promotion of your Kickstarter campaign.

Thankfully, there are several free or low-cost resources that can handle most of the back-end work and still present a nice basic site to your backers or potential backers. I review two choices in the following sections and outline some options to consider for each.

 In Chapter 3, I discuss building a solid budget, and one line item to consider is any cost for constructing, maintaining, and promoting an individual website for your project.

WordPress.com

WordPress.com is by far the most popular and widely used website for free website creation. This site enables you to choose from different predesigned themes for your site. Each theme offers a different overall look and feel for the finished site. Figure 10-14 shows a small sampling of the available WordPress themes.

Some of the themes are free, meaning you only have to create an account to begin the design process, and others are premium themes, meaning you pay a fee to download and use the features of the theme.

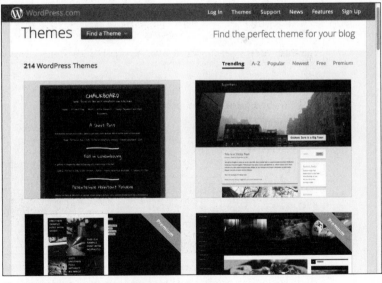

Figure 10-14: Sample WordPress.com themes.

Most of the technology behind WordPress is drag-and-drop, which means you work within a visual interface and don't have to know HTML or other web-based languages to build a website.

I recommend that you start by reviewing the free themes to get a sense of how WordPress.com works, because these themes are simplest to use. After you feel a bit more confident, try using a Premium theme, which may have advanced features such as

✔ Animated graphics

✔ Photo sliders or slideshows that constantly update

✔ Sidebars or widgets that you can customize

✔ Custom backgrounds or fonts

✔ Different selections for main posts, aside posts, and callouts

Figure 10-15 below shows a sample web page using the Avid theme, specifically designed for photo-heavy blogs.

Figure 10-15: Sample blog using Avid WordPress theme.

WordPress.com hosts your website for free, which means the files you create via the visual interface are stored on the WordPress web servers. (Your website files must reside on a web server so that your website visitors' browsers can access the files when visitors type in your site's web address.)

When you use WordPress.com to host your site, your default website address (also known as a *domain name*) is www.wordpress.com/YOURADDRESSHERE.com. You can keep that address or create your own via a process called *domain registration*. Using the default address is faster and easier than registering your own domain, but I recommend spending the time and money (between $7–$39 per year depending on what you register) creating your own website address. For example, the website I created for my Finding 40 Kickstarter project is www.finding40.net. Having a web address that matches my project name keeps the branding for my project simple and focused and helps people interested in my project find it online.

To use your own domain name with a WordPress.com website, here are the overall steps to follow:

1. **Visit a domain name registrar to make sure the name you want is available and follow the registrar's steps to reserve your desired domain name.**

   You can register any name you like as long as no one else has taken it. As I mention earlier, you most likely want your domain name to match your project name. The two best-known and least expensive registrars are www.1and1.com and www.GoDaddy.com. WordPress.com also provides a domain registration service through its store. You can also check out providers such as www.name.com and www.namecheap.com for website domain services.

2. **After you register your domain, point your WordPress.com blog to your domain.**

   As this book goes to press, you have to pay about $20 per year to use your own domain name with a WordPress.com blog or website. Click the Store link in your WordPress.com dashboard and follow the instructions to add a domain.

For more details about using WordPress to create a website, check out the WordPress articles at Dummies.com or the book *WordPress For Dummies,* 5th Edition, by Lisa Sabin-Wilson.

The more advanced you get with a WordPress site, the more you can add in, including a shopping solution (allowing people to buy directly from your site), ticket sales, and other embedded advertisements and commerce opportunities.

Blogger

Blogger is part of Google, and like the name implies, it is mostly designed for creating fairly basic blogs. Go to www.blogger.com and click the button that says Take a Quick Tour to get a basic sense of how this service works.

As with WordPress, you can design a page visually by choosing and customizing themes. You don't need to know HTML to use Blogger; it's easy for a novice website creator to use.

As with WordPress, you can host your blog on Blogger for free, meaning you'll have an address that is preceded with http:// blogspot.YOURBLOGNAME.com. If you want to create a blog with your own unique web address, register your domain before you start your blog. Doing so will make setting up your blog easier than trying to change the default blogspot name later.

Figure 10-16 shows a sample of the Blogger Dashboard.

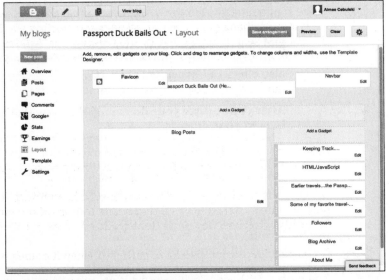

Figure 10-16: Dashboard inside a Blogger page.

Sites created using Blogger will not have as many theme options available as the hundreds of WordPress themes. Blogger themes are usually simpler and designed for more basic photo sharing and blogging. Of course, there is an entire aftermarket where you can buy or download other Blogger themes and expand the functionality of your Blogspot page — but again, consider how much time and energy you can put into this part of your project, and plan accordingly.

It's also important to remember that Blogger, as part of Google, may not remain free forever or may change significantly over time; be sure to have a back up plan in place if a free website service should suddenly become unavailable.

Tumblr

This popular blog creation website currently boasts over 100 million users worldwide, including Kickstarter, which uses Tumblr for its own blog mentioned earlier in this chapter. Tumblr (www. tumblr.com) users can create a site also using drag-and-drop technology similar to WordPress and Blogger, and the Tumblr community has better search functions to tag your blog with keywords, making it easier for anyone who just comes to the main Tumblr web page to find your Tumblr page.

There are countless other tools out there for building websites; the list is always changing. To peruse some of the most recent offerings, try a Google search for "Free Web Site Creation" or "Making Your Own Web Site." You'll see more choices than you ever thought possible.

Taking Great Photos

As you've seen throughout this book, many of the most successful Kickstarter campaigns give backers a real sense of what they're supporting — often through strong and clear photographs.

Because the Internet is such a visual medium, anything you post as part of your Kickstarter campaign needs to pop off the monitor or tablet and grab the viewer's attention as much as possible.

Here are a few basic tips I have gathered when it comes to shooting and posting photographs as part of your Kickstarter campaign:

✔ Keep your photos as uncluttered as possible, focusing on the Kickstarter item or descriptive point itself.

✔ If necessary, use an image editor to crop or otherwise remove elements that take away from your main message. For example, if you took a photo of a building you're trying to convert to a theater and people in the background detract from the image, think about removing them from the image before posting it to your Kickstarter campaign page or elsewhere.

✔ Bright, colorful images will pop off the screen; black and white images will meld with text.

✔ When you post the photo of yourself in your profile, pick a photo that really shows your personality and face. If possible, do a head and shoulders shot or simple head shot.

✔ If you are producing something that will end up being a collection (like the Pebble E-Paper Watch that came in multiple colors), post photographs of each item individually, as well as a group shot so people can see the finished collection.

✔ Remember to lower the resolution before posting! If you take a photo with a digital camera (or even your smartphone) as part of your campaign, each of those individual photos might be a 2MB (or bigger) file. If you upload them directly as-is into your Kickstarter Dashboard, they'll be so large that they'll load sluggishly when someone tries to view them. Use your photo-editing tool to save a lower-resolution version of the image and upload that smaller picture! See `Dummies.com` for tips and articles about saving and optimizing images for the web. Also, be sure to always keep your original high-resolution photo on file; you will need that for any printed materials.

Promoting Your Project or Event

In Chapter 6, I discuss the idea of hosting or participating in a promotional event to get the word out about your Kickstarter campaign and upcoming deadline. There are several tools that can be helpful when promoting an event of this type:

✔ `Eventbrite.com` is a catch-all event-listing and planning website, with a huge calendar of events searchable by neighborhood, type of event, date, and cost. Anyone can post details of an event here simply by creating a free Eventbrite account. Eventbrite also lets guests pre-purchase tickets to your event (if you're charging a fee) and shows how many tickets are left if you've limited the number of attendees. Additionally, you can use Eventbrite to e-mail potential attendees and promote your event through an integrated e-mail tool.

✔ `Zvents.com` is another free event-listing site, designed to be more of a calendar of events and less of an integrated event-management site. If you're hosting a promotional event to highlight your Kickstarter campaign, this is another opportunity to get the word out and attract attendees. Again, all the events are searchable by neighborhood, date, and category.

✔ You may know of Evite.com through birthday party or wedding shower planning, but did you know you can use it also to create a virtual event relating to your Kickstarter deadline? Invite others to join your event and help you reach your goal. Figure 10-17 below shows a sample of the many Evite templates that are appropriate to fundraising.

Figure 10-17: Sample fundraising templates on Evite.

Index

• A •

About You tab, 86, 93–94, 96
Abram, Carolyn (author)
  Facebook For Dummies,
    105
Accepted status, 99–100
Account tab, 86, 94–95
Activity icon (App
  interface), 137, 141
Add Another Backer Reward
  tile, 91
add-ons, 71
Adler, Charles (Kickstarter
  cofounder), 6
advertising, 54, 119–123,
  180–183, 189
aftermarket docks (for
  iPhone), 43–45
all-or-nothing approach, 7, 8,
  57, 119, 145
Amazon, credit card
  processing fees, 48, 89
Amazon Payments account,
  83, 94–95, 146
Android, 34, 133
Animoto, 31
AP Stylebook, 183, 184
Apple
  fan base, 125, 126
  iPhone Elevation Dock
    Campaign. *See* iPhone,
    Elevation Dock
    Campaign
  standard Apple Dock, 44
approval process
  polished video as easing
    of, 29
  preparing for, 96–97
  as step in crowdfunding
    process, 16
  timeline for, 99
archive, of all materials,
  notes, and files, 146
Art category, 35
artists' nights, 123–124
artist's signature, as reward,
  163–164

audio, 27, 93
audio multimedia tool, 93
author's signature, as
  reward, 163–164

• B •

backer goals, 61
backer perks, 71. *See also*
  rewards
Backer Questions, 13
Backer Report, 111–114,
  151–154, 157
backer rewards. *See* rewards
BackerKit, 174–175
backers
  advantages of Kickstarter
    to, 8–9
  bad sentiments among, 74
  as characters in movie,
    book, or TV show,
    162–163
  contacting, 113–117
  creating a compelling call
    to action for, 102, 146,
    183
  encouraging community
    with, 147
  estimating number needed
    at different funding
    levels, 60
  figuring out specific backer
    goals, 61
  to launch as compared to
    funding entire project,
    53
  making of as heroes of
    project, 166–167
  meeting of in person,
    167–168
  potential backers, 7, 58–59,
    102–111
  promoting deadline to,
    117–119
  relationship with, 16–17
  rewards for. *See* rewards
  surveying, 154–157
  thanking, 61, 62, 146, 147

  unhappy ones as very
    vocal, 28, 79
  updates to. *See* updates
bad press, 73, 74
The Bargain (comic
  campaign), 36
Barrow, Colin (author)
  Business Plans For Dummies,
    3rd Edition, 178
Basic Pizza (restaurant),
  123–124
Basics tab, 86, 87, 89
bio/biography, 23–24, 94
bit parts, rewarding backers
  with, 164–165
BlackBerry, 34
Blogger, 190–191
Blogspot page, 191
Bluetooth, 80
BMP (file format), 87, 93
bold text tool, 92
Boutenko, Sergei
  (filmmaker), 185, 186
Bplans, 178
Break.com, posting of video
  on, 110
budget
  estimating back pledges, 57
  estimating in general, 48
  estimating production
    costs, 53
  formatting of, 75
  resources for developing,
    176–177
budget overages, as example
  of challenge, 28
Build Your Business Plan
  tool (SBA), 178
Burlew, Rich (comic creator),
  64, 67, 69
business page, on Facebook,
  108
business plan, resources for
  developing, 177–179
Business Plans For Dummies,
  3rd Edition (Tiffany,
  Peterson, and Barrow),
  178

• C •

call to action
  creating a compelling one, 102–104, 130, 146, 183
  tweeting about, 108
campaign. *See also* promotion
  contacting backers through Kickstarter, 113–117
  contacting owners of successful campaigns, 147
  contacting potential backers, 102–111
  creating a compelling call to action for, 102, 146, 183
  handling struggling or unsuccessful one, 145–147
  launching, 99–101
  learning from other campaigns, 147, 175–176
  looking at from new angle, 146
  posting of on Facebook, 104–108
  posting updates. *See* updates
  posting video on video-sharing sites, 110–111
  sending message to backers, 113–114
  sending personal e-mails, 103
  tracking backers, 111–113
  tweeting of on Twitter, 108–109
categories, 23, 35–42
challenges, 28–29
changes, when allowed, when not allowed, 84, 89, 101
charities, Kickstarter as not a fundraising tool for, 10–11
charting/calculation software, 48
Chen, Perry (musician), 6
Choosing an Image from Your Computer link, 87
CNNMoney, 73
collaboration, 26

Comics category, 36
ComicsBeat, 67, 68
comma-separate values (CSV) format, 153
commission, 8
communication tools, 114
community
  building of around your project, 148–150
  fostering of offline, 149–150
  as potential backers, 58
  sense of, 9
  sustaining of after project ends, 148–149
community guidelines, 15
concept, project, 7
contact list, 58
content, that is not allowed, 11
Cook, Lucas (musician), 163–164
Cooking with Fire: The Disaster Cookbook campaign, 42
Copy Blogger, 181
copy editing, 179–180
copywriting, resources on, 180–182
costs. *See also* project costs
  estimating production costs, 53
  hard costs, 49
  of rewards, 15
  sources of information for, 52
countdown to end of campaign, 106, 118–119
cover, featuring backers on your, as reward, 159–160
coworkers, as potential backers, 58
Craigslist.org, 52
Create a Survey button, 114, 152, 154–155
creative control, 9–10
Creator Notifications (App interface), 139
Creator Questions, 12
credit card processing fees, Amazon, 48, 89
Creita campaign, 185, 186
crowdfunding, 1, 5–6, 15–17
CV, 23–24

• D •

DailyMotion.com, posting of video on, 110
Dance category, 36
dashboard
  being directed to, 86, 101
  icon on iPhone app, 136, 137, 140
  individual reward box, 90
  overview, 141
  use of to message backers, 147
  visual of, 87
date-dependent items, 75–77
day job, working around, 77
days remaining, 7
deadline
  advantages of, 8
  missing of, as example of challenge, 28
  promotion of, 16, 117–119
delays
  equipment rental as potential for, 76
  as example of a challenge, 28
  iPhone Elevation Dock campaign, 79–80
  Pebble E-Paper Watch campaign, 81
  Printrbot campaign, 74
  staffing as potential for, 76
  troubleshooting of, 16
delivery
  estimated delivery date, 77–78
  examples of projects very late or not yet delivered, 73–74
  of rewards, 151–157
Description box, 90
Design category, 37
design improvement, 42
Dig South Interactive Conference and Expo campaign, example of bringing out-of-town backer to event, as reward, 170–171
digital giving, 1
dinner parties, as rewards, 167–168
Discover icon (App interface), 137
display ads, 120

domain name, 189
domain registration, 189
donations, estimating
    potential, 57–64
Double Fine Adventure
    campaign, 73–74
Dummies.com, 75, 178
Dunay, Paul (author)
    *Facebook Marketing For
    Dummies*, 107
duration (of project), 23, 26,
    89, 97, 100–101

• E •

Edit Project, 112
The Elements of Style (Strunk
    Jr. and White), 179,
    180
Elevation Dock campaign,
    42, 43–45, 79–80,
    125–127
ElevationLab, 44, 125, 126
e-mail messages
    countdown emphasized in,
        119, 146
    individual thank-you to
        each backer, 147
    with project approval, 100
    sending personal ones,
        103–104
ending date, 100–101,
    117–119
equipment, rental/purchase,
    48, 51, 76
Eventbrite.com, 192
events
    bringing of out-of-town
        backer to event as
        reward, 170–171
    hosting of to educate
        potential backers,
        120, 123–125
Evite.com, 193
Excel For Dummies (Harvey),
    176
Excel spreadsheet, 48–51,
    153, 176

• F •

Facebook
    buying advertisement on,
        119–121
    countdown emphasized in
        posts on, 146

getting started on, 105
linking to, 94
News Feed, 104
The Order of the Stock
    (comic) on, 67, 68
posting promotion of
    campaign on, 104
promoting your post on,
    119
sample posts announcing
    campaign, 105–106
using a Facebook business
    page, 107–108
as way to provide link to
    campaign page, 9
your community on as
    potential backers, 58
Facebook Connect, 85, 93
Facebook For Dummies
    (Abram), 105
*Facebook Marketing For
    Dummies* (Haydon,
    Dunay, and Krueger),
    107
Facebook Timeline, 142
fairs/festivals, participation
    in, 54
family, as potential backers,
    58
fan base, 64, 67–69
FAQs (Frequently Asked
    Questions), 12–13
Fashion category, 37
fee (percentage) of funds
    raised, 12
Fee check box, 91
file formats for images, 87,
    93
Film & Video category, 38
The Finding 40 Project
    campaign
    backer levels, 60
    call to action, 102
    example of home-cooked
        meal as reward,
        167–168
    Facebook page, 107
    learning from, 127–131
    personal e-mail example,
        103–104
    promotion of deadline, 118
    in Publishing category, 40
    website URL, 189
fine print, 12–15
Fitton, Laura (author)
    Twitter For Dummies, 105
food, as rewards, 167–168
Food category, 38, 42

formatting
    of budget, 75
    of long project description,
        27, 92
    of project video, 91
Fresh (theater campaign), 41
full project description, 24.
    See also long project
    description
"Fund My Life" projects, 11
funding duration, 101
Funding Goal box, 89
funding your own project, as
    against the rules, 146
fundraising goal
    all-or-nothing approach to, 7
    compare yours to others',
        57
    of Double Fine Adventure
        campaign, 73
    double-checking, 97
    entering of, 89
    figuring out of, 15–16
    of *The Finding 40 Project*
        campaign, 130
    guidelines for, 47–48
    of iPhone Elevation Dock
        campaign, 79
    lowering of without
        dramatically changing
        project scope, 60
    minimum, 8, 16
    of *The Order of the Stick*
        campaign, 65
    of Pebble E-Paper Watch
        campaign, 80–81
    of Printrbot campaign, 74
    setting of, 14–16, 23, 60–62
    of Spaghetti & Meatballs,
        117–118
    of VOTA campaign, 160
FunnyOrDie.com, posting of
    video on, 110

• G •

Games category, 39
Generate Your Report
    button, 114, 152
geographic area focus, 26
GIF (file format), 87, 93
Gizmodo (website), 126
goal, fundraising. *See*
    fundraising goal
goal, primary, 24, 29, 35, 36
goals, backer, 61
GoDaddy.com, 189

Google
  Blogger, 190, 191
  Picasa, 33, 147
GoogleVideo.com, posting of
    video on, 110
graphic novel industry, 1
Gruen, Michael (author)
  Twitter For Dummies, 105
guidelines, 11
Guidelines link, 14–15

• H •

*Hack: More Stories from
    a Chicago Cab*
    (Samarov), 149
hard costs, 49
Harvey, Greg (author)
  Excel For Dummies, 176
Haydon, John (author)
  *Facebook Marketing For
    Dummies*, 107
HD resolution, 30
heading text tool, 92
hero worship, making
    backers heroes of
    your project, as
    reward, 166–167
holidays, handling of, 16,
    100–101
home-cooked meals, as
    rewards, 167–168
Hopkins, Casey (designer),
    44
HTML, 188, 190
The Huffington Post, 176
humor, posting of humorous
    videos, 110
Hyper-Heroes campaign,
    example of making
    backer hero of,
    166–167

• I •

icons, explained, 3
image multimedia tool, 93
image-editing program, 31, 87
images. *See* photos/images
iMovie, 30
Indiegogo (crowdfunding
    site), 11
industry, as potential
    backers, 58–59
industry factors, 16
integrated video camera, 34

Internet, buying
    advertisement
    on, 119, 121–123
Introduction to Survey
    option, 156
iPad, Kickstarter iPhone
    app, 133
iPhone
  Elevation Dock campaign,
    42, 43–45, 79–80,
    125–127
  integrated video camera, 34
  Kickstarter app, 16, 112,
    117, 133–144
  logging in and out, 136–137
  managing campaign from,
    140–144
italic text tool, 92
Iva Jean campaign, 37

• J •

JPEG (file format), 87, 93

• K •

key elements, 21–22
keywords, 110, 175, 191
Kickstarter. *See also specific
    topics*
  account setup, 84–86
  advantages of, 8–10
  authors' pages, 158
  campaign page, 7
  history of, 6
  home page, 12–13
  how it makes its money, 8
  keeping up with, 157–158
  school (virtual school), 14
  statistics on launched
    projects, 6–7
  URL, 108, 110
  what it does and doesn't
    fund, 10–11
Kickstarter App interface,
    137–140
Kickstarter Basics, 12
Kickstarter Blog, 157, 158
Kickstarter Category drop-
    down menu, 88
Kickstarter For Dummies
    (website), 3
The Kickstarter Tumblr
    page, 174
Kickstarter-specific
    resources, 173–175
Kicktraq, 173–174

killer content, how to write,
    181
knowledge/technical skill,
    lack of, as example of
    challenge, 28
Krizan, Kim (writer)
  Before Sunrise (movie), 10
  Before Sunset (movie), 10
Krueger, Richard (author)
  *Facebook Marketing For
    Dummies*, 107

• L •

Launch button, 101
launch party, 54
lessons learned, 146
licenses, 48, 51, 76
link text tool, 92
list text tool, 92
LivePlan, 178, 179
location (in About You tab),
    94
location, geographic area
    focus, 26, 120
login, 85–86
long project description,
    26–29
Love Thy Nature
    (documentary
    campaign), 38
Lucas, Austin (musician), 39

• M •

marketing, expense
    category, 49, 54, 120
marketing fee, 8
Mashable, 175–176
Me icon, 111
media. *See also specific
    media*
media, choosing of to
    support your
    description, 27
media kit, 122
Media Upload icons, 115
Meetup, 150
Message All link, 114, 152
messages
  to backers in a reward tier,
    114
  to an individual backer,
    114
  viewing and replying to,
    via Kickstarter App,
    140–141

Messages function (App interface), 139
Microsoft, 30
Microsoft Excel, 153, 176
Microsoft Project, 75
minimum goal amount, 8, 16
Monster.com, 52
MP3 format, 93
MP4 format, 93
multimedia, tools for inserting, 92–93
Multiple Choice Question option, 156–157
music, as element of video, 31, 32
Music category, 39

• *N* •

name (in About You tab), 93
naming rights, as rewards, 162
News Feed (on Facebook), 104
newspaper, buying advertisement in, 120–123
nonactive buttons (in Backer Report), 114

• *O* •

Oblivion web series, 164, 165
offline, fostering of community via, 149–150
1and1.com, 189
one-on-one conversations, with potential backers, 102
online interfaces, 84
Open Office Calc, 153
open-ended questions (in survey), 156
OpenOffice Calc, 176–177
The Order of the Stock (comic campaign), 36, 64–71
Original Sins: Trade Secrets of a Femme Fatale campaign, 10

• *P* •

password, Kickstarter account, 85
Patch.com, 150

payment account, 83, 94–95, 146
Pebble E-Paper Watch campaign, 22, 23, 76, 79, 80–81
percentage (fee) of funds raised, 8, 12
performance, tickets to as rewards, 165–166
permits, 48, 51, 53, 76
personal time constraints, as example of a challenge, 28
Peterson, Steven D. (author) *Business Plans For Dummies*, 3rd Edition, 178
Photography category, 40
Photoshop/Photoshop Elements, 87
photos/images
    in 4.3 aspect ratio, 22, 87
    posting of on Facebook page, 106
    sizes of, 87–88, 93, 192
    to support your description, 27
    taking great photos, 191–192
Picasa, 33, 147
Pinterest, 58, 94
pitfalls, potential, 28
Pledge Amount box, 90
pledges
    estimating, 57
    overview, 7, 8
    soliciting upgrades to, 124, 146
Plunder game campaign, example of unique reward, 162–163
PNG (file format), 87, 93
Pollyanna Cowgirl Records Podcast campaign, example of unique reward, 162
Poston, Leslie (author) *Twitter For Dummies*, 105
Post Update function, 79, 112
Post Update tab, 115
"Powered by Green Smoothies" campaign, 185, 186
press releases, resources for writing, 182–184
Preview, 89, 97
Printrbot campaign, 74

private viewing option for updates, 116
product length, 26
product samples, 54
production
    considerations about in creating realistic timeline, 76
    costs, 53
    expense category, 49, 52–53
production quotes, 76
professional organizations, as potential backers, 146
Profile icon (App interface), 137
profile photo, 93
Prohibited Uses (Kickstarter guidelines), 11
project
    building, 14
    concept of, 7
    defining, 14, 15
    description of, 22, 24–29, 92–94
    Kickstarter as fundraising tool for, 11
    page, example of, 111
    prepping to start, 21–24
    profile of, 86–89
    story of, telling, 91–93
    transforming your passion into, 20–21
    video of. *See* video, project
Project 2013 For Dummies (Snyder), 75
Project Activity page, 151, 154
project costs
    examining costs of other campaigns, 54–57
    figuring, 47–57
    listing individual expenses, 49–50
    outlining broad expense categories, 48–49
    trying to estimate, 50–54
Project Description box, 27, 92
Project Duration box, 89
Project Guidelines, 85–86
Project Image area, 87
Project Location box, 89
Project of the Day link, 125
Project Title box, 88
Project Update screen, 115

Projecteo campaign, 37
project-management tool, 75
Projects You Back (App
    interface), 139
promotion
    of deadline, 16, 117–119
    expense category, 54
    as key element, 14
    paying to promote,
        119–125
    pledge upgrade
        promotions, 124
    of project or event,
        resources on, 192–193
    of project to people in
        your geographic area,
        120
promotional copy, 180–182
PRWeb, 183, 184
PSD (file format), 87
Public Relations Society of
    America (PRSA),
    183
public user name, 85
public viewing option for
    updates, 116
publicity, 180–182
Publishers Weekly, 1
Publishing category, 40, 42
*Publishing the +5 of Eating
    Cookbook* campaign, 42

● **Q** ●

Q&A section, 128
questions, FAQ (Frequently
    Asked Questions),
    12–13

● **R** ●

raffle events, 124
raw material, unable to
    get, as example of
    challenge, 28
Rdio (audio-sharing site), 93
research/licenses/permits,
    48, 51
residency requirements, 12
résumé, 23–24
review, preparing for, 96–97
Review tab, 86, 96
reward fulfillment, 14
rewards
    cost of, 15
    creating, 14

delivery of, 16–17, 151–157,
    174
evaluating potential
    reward levels, 59–61
examples of creative and
    personalized, 63–64,
    69–71
examples of unique
    rewards, 159–171
as listed on campaign
    page, 7
The Order of the Stock
    campaign, 71
overview, 24
setting up, 61–64, 90–91
staggering of reward dates,
    78–79
surveying backers, 154
Rewards tab, 86, 90
risks, 28–29

● **S** ●

Sabin-Wilson, Lisa (author)
    WordPress For Dummies,
        5th Edition, 189
Samarov, Dimitri (writer)
    *Hack: More Stories from a
        Chicago Cab*, 149
Sample Theater campaign,
    41
SBA (Small Business
    Administration), 178
scale-up issues, 74
Screwtape campaign,
    example of tickets to
    production of, 165–166
search tags, 110
second family (coworkers),
    as potential backers, 58
Send Message icon, 114
sense of community, 9
Settings function (App
    interface), 139
setup process, 16
shipping options, 91
short blurb, 22, 110
Short Blurb box, 88
short project description,
    22, 24–26
short URL, 108
show, tickets to as rewards,
    165–166
signing your work, as reward,
    163–164
single-word description, 24

Small Business Adminis
    tration (SBA), 178
smartphone
    Kickstarter-like apps for, 112
    as tool for creating video,
        34
Smugmug (photo-sharing
    site), 147
Snyder, Cynthia (author)
    Project 2013 For Dummies,
        75
social media, 148. *See also*
    Facebook; Twitter
Social Notifications (App
    interface), 139, 140
SoundCloud (audio-sharing
    site), 93
Spaghetti & Meatballs
    campaign, 117, 118
spell checking, 92
sponsored story ads, 120
spreadsheet, 48–51, 153, 176
staff hours, 48, 52, 76
status, Accepted, 99–100
stories, learning from other
    Kickstarter stories,
    175–176
story, project's, telling of,
    91–93
Story tab, 86, 91
Strickler, Yancey (Kickstarter
    cofounder), 6
Strunk, William, Jr. (author)
    The Elements of Style, 179
Submit for Review, 97
subscriptions, as rewards,
    169
Sugar Knife Marshmallows
    campaign, 38
survey feature, 154–157. *See
    also* Create a Survey
    button

● **T** ●

targeted advertising, 120
Technology category, 41
temporary help, 48, 52
terms and conditions, 11,
    12–15
text tools, 92
thank-yous, to backers, 61,
    62, 146, 147
Theater category, 41
TheNextWeb (website), 126
thesaurus, 182

ThinkMap Visual Thesaurus, 182
Thirty-Two magazine, example of subscription as reward, 169
This Week in Kickstarter, 157
tickets to your show, as rewards, 165–166
TIF (file format), 87
Tiffany, Paul (author)
  Business Plans For Dummies, 3rd Edition, 178
Timber and Stone (game campaign), 39
time, running out of, as example of challenge, 28
time constraints, as example of challenge, 28
timeframe, 23, 26
timeline
  creating, 75–78
  experiencing success and then delays, 79–81
  importance of being realistic with, 75
  setting of, 16
  staggering reward dates, 78–79
TinyDuino campaign, 41
Trailer Food Diaries: Cookbook campaign, 42
troubleshooting, possible delays, 16
t-shirts, as rewards, 161–162
Tumblr (blog creation website), 191
tweets, 105, 108
Twitter
  countdown emphasized in feeds on, 146
  getting started on, 105
  linking to, 94
  sample tweets announcing campaign, 109
  as style for short blurb, 22
  tweeting about your campaign, 108–109

as way to provide link to campaign page, 9
your community on as potential backers, 58
Twitter For Dummies (Fitton, Gruen, and Poston), 105

• U •

unique selling point, 24–26
United Kingdom (U.K.), requirements for Kickstarter participation in, 12
United States (U.S.), requirements for Kickstarter participation in, 12
unlink text tool, 92
unsuccessful campaign, following up on, 146–147
updates
  as key element, 14
  posting of, 114–117, 149
  posting of on Kickstarter app, 142–144
  private view option for, 116
  public view option for, 116
  selecting how to receive, 139
upload tools, 92
Upload Video button, 91
URL, short, 108, 110
user name, Kickstarter account, 85

• V •

vacation package, as reward, 170
video, project
  on campaign page, 7
  choosing tools for, 30–34
  as key element, 22
  length of, 30
  making a compelling one, 29–34
  outlining content for, 29–30
  overview, 14

possible format issues, 91
raw materials for, 30
to support your description, 27
uploading, 91
Video button, 93
video multimedia tool, 92–93
video-sharing sites, 110–111
Vimeo, 93, 110
virtual school (Kickstarter school), 14
VOTA campaign, example of unique reward, 160

• W •

walk-on roles, rewarding backers with, 164–165
WAV format, 93
weather/seasons/special events, conflicts with, as examples of challenges, 28
web links, 27
website, building/ maintaining, 54, 185–191
What Is Kickstarter? link, 12, 13
White, E. B. (author)
  The Elements of Style, 179
Windows Movie Maker, 30
Wire Magazine, 44
word usage, resources on, 179–180
WordPress For Dummies, 5th Edition (Sabin-Wilson), 189
WordPress.com, 187–189
Wordy, 179–180
writing resources, 179–180

• Y •

YouTube, 93, 110
YouTube Video Editor, 32–33

• Z •

Zvents.com, 192